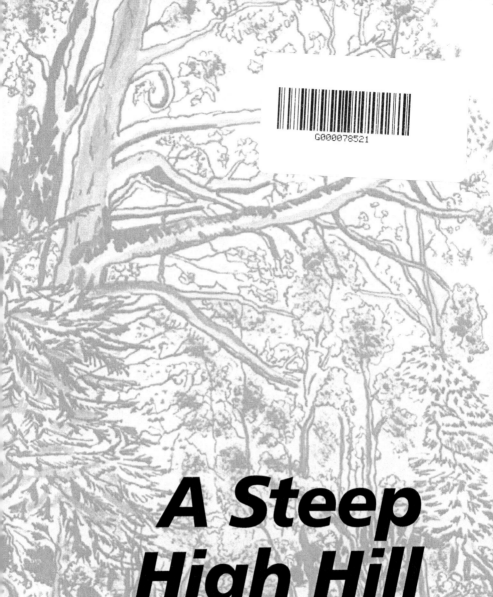

A Steep High Hill

Blue Bell Hill Village

Edwina Kissick BSc

A Steep High Hill

2nd Edition   April 2011
1st Edition   April 1996
© 1996–2011 Edwina Kissick Estate
ISBN 978-1-8718141-5-6

The publisher is grateful to Aylesford Parish Council and the Blue Bell Hill Preservation Group for financial support for this revised edition.

Proceeds from the sale of this book will support the publication of a new largely photographic history of Blue Bell Hill, Walderslade and Lordswood telling the stories of these settlements from where Miss Kissick's books ended. All of these books are sold on a non-profit making basis to support the knowledge and understanding of the area by the local community.

Designed and typeset by Imagic Design, Chatham, Kent
01634 864017 • www.imagic-design.co.uk

Trade Distribution by Roadmaster Publishing, PO Box 176, Chatham, Kent ME5 9AQ
01634 862843 • email roadmasterpublishing@blueyonder.co.uk

A Steep High Hill

Blue Bell Hill Village

Edwina Kissick BSc

A Steep High Hill — Blue Bell Hill

Introduction

I have no qualifications to write a history of Blue Bell Hill, other than 60 years' acquaintance with the area and sufficient interest to do the work involved. If the historians tell me I've got it wrong, I shall accept reproof. If anyone else tells me it's wrong, I shall argue with them, if for no better reason than that I enjoy arguing.

We are told that, when embarking upon a local history project, the aim should be clearly stated. Mine was simple. I set out to find out what I could about the history of the area in which I live. It did not look very promising, consisting largely of dry chalk valleys, 20th century housing estates and extensive woodlands, and I did not expect to obtain much information. In fact, there was so much that the project soon split into two. The area to the west of me — Blue Bell Hill — took over. The area to the east of me — Walderslade — remains to be done.

Similarly, I did not consciously define my area of study. It gradually defined itself as the Blue Bell Hill Ward of Aylesford parish, plus the old North Ward of Burham parish, which was transferred into Aylesford in 1988. This gave an area stretching from the Pilgrims' Way in the south, to the B2097 in the north, and from the parish boundary along Forest Drive/Tunbury Avenue in the east to a vague western boundary running from somewhere along Common Road to Great Culand. I have cut off the study at the 1939–1945 war. This will disappoint some people, but so many local residents volunteered information about the post-war period that the book would have become top-heavy if I had included it. I suggest that this needs a book of another type.

Much of the evidence for the earlier history has come as small grains from scattered sources. I have tried to make it clear:

a) When I am presenting evidence;

b) When I am reasoning on a basis of the evidence;

c) When I am reasoning on the basis of an hypothesis already put forward but which cannot be irrefutably proven (especially in Chapter Seven);

The area around Blue Bell Hill in 1930.

(Modern road alignments are shown for reference.)

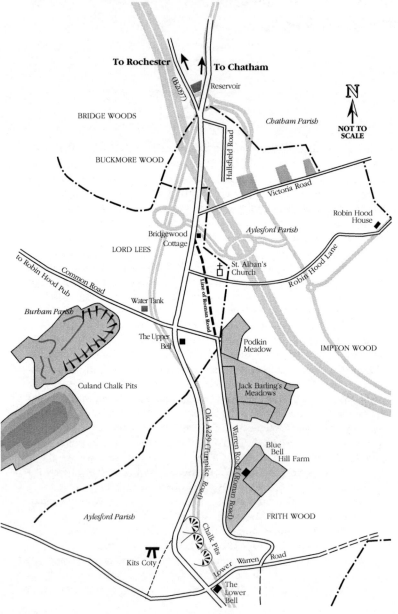

d) When I am merely speculating.

I have enjoyed doing the work, and I hope that some people, at least, will derive interest from reading the book. If I have done nothing else, I have given the 20th century village of Blue Bell Hill a history of its own.

Acknowledgements

I am indebted to all the people who, wittingly or otherwise, have supplied information for this book. I have tried to include all of them in the bibliographies at the ends of chapters or, occasionally, within the text. I apologise if I have inadvertently omitted anyone. I offer thanks to:

Mr E ("Pat") Sandford (Blue Bell Hill Lime Works); Mrs Goodayle (Kits Coty Estate); Mrs J Brennan (Blue Bell Hill Farm); Mr B Gray (shops in the developing village; he also provided newspaper cuttings and other papers relating to the early fêtes and to the history of St Alban's Church); and Mr N White (Kits Coty Estate — he also offered me access to original documentation relating to the auction of the estate and to the Little Farm).

I express my great appreciation of the unfailing courtesy and patience of the staff of Kent County Council's Archives Office, including the men in brown overalls who carry great tonnages of documents, encrusted with the grime of ages, from the secret recesses of the Archives Office to the Search Room. My thanks also to the staff of the Local History Library at Springfield (before it was closed) and the central reference libraries at Chatham, Maidstone, Rochester and Gillingham, for help in locating sundry books, maps and old newspapers. Also, to the Clerk of the Records at the House of Lords Record Office, for help in locating the Turnpike Acts, and Mr P D Wilkinson, CEng, MICE, MIWEM (Mid Kent Water Company); Mr G Setterfield (Southern Water Authority) for providing information about the reservoirs.

I express my special thanks to Mrs Madge Johnson for supplying the photographs of Old Blue Bell Hill village; to Paddy and Michael McGuire for their careful reading and correction of the initial badly-typed script; and to my good friends, Percy and Hazel Harryman, for supplying much information and encouragement, and to Percy for permission to use the past minutes of Blue Bell Hill Village Hall and the Rate-payers' Association: I deeply regret that he did not live to read the finished book.

I am indebted to Macmillan General Books and Mrs Dorothy Gibson for permission to reproduce the poem Lament by W W Gibson, at the end of Chapter Eleven.

Finally, I wish to express my most sincere thanks to Mrs J Allonby for providing and giving permission to use the delightful black and white sketches, including the illustration on the cover and the Upper Bell, and above all to Ms Heather Kavanagh, without whose know-how, freely given over many hours, this book would probably not have seen the light of day.

Notes on the second edition
Heather Kavanagh, October 2010

Since *A Steep High Hill* was first published in 1996, it became the habit of the author to include an errata and amendments sheet with each copy. As the original publisher, and holder of the electronic files for the book, I promised myself I would eventually update it to incorporate the amendments and add metric equivalents for weights and measures quoted, perhaps with a view to publishing a revised second edition.

Edwina Kissick sadly died in 2009. Before her death, we had published the volume on Walderslade alluded to in her introduction above, *Walderslade — the wooded valley*, and she had begun work on a similar history of Lordswood. I have her computer here, which does contain the seed of such a book, but I feel it will need the skills of a proper historian to nurture it further.

As the original publisher of both this and the Walderslade book, I had discussed with Eddie — she always preferred to be called that over the full version of her Christian name — the idea of producing a revised and updated issue of *A Steep High Hill*, and also the possibility of getting much of the information from both books into a web site. Understandably, she felt that electronic forms of her published materials were beyond her understanding, and we'd left things that I would work towards a web site in due course, with her blessing.

Obviously, with her passing, such matters have transferred to her executors and estate. I write these notes in the hope we can resolve matters in a way that ensures Eddie's work can be shared in the widest possible sense.

I have, therefore, updated the manuscript with the corrections Eddie made. I have revised the maps to help readers identify how the area has changed over the years. References to places in relation to modern landmarks have been checked and updated where possible, especially since the M2 and its junction with the A229 has been extensively remodelled since the book was originally written.

Finally, a note on currency values. In the original edition of *A Steep High Hill*, we had shown decimal equivalents of pounds, shillings and pence using the direct equivalency chosen when the "old money" changed to "new" at the start of the 1970s. One shilling, therefore, equated to five new pence, two shillings to ten new pence, and so on. Sadly, this form of conversion gives no idea to modern eyes of the actual value of pre-decimal money. A good working wage in the first quarter of the 20th century was something like 25 shillings a week, which would equate to £1.25 in "new" money using the direct conversion. This gives a false impression that the cost of living then was much lower than today. I prefer to consider such conversions in a different way by using the cost of a loaf of bread. Very roughly, today the cost of an average loaf of bread is about £1. Over much of the historical period covered in this volume, a loaf of bread would have been of the order of a penny. We might therefore equate one old penny to one 21st century pound sterling, so our 25 shillings per week becomes a more understandable £300. Please bear this in mind as you read this book.

(For those too young to know, including myself, there were 12 pence in a shilling and 20 shillings, or 240 pence, in a pound. A penny was, until 1960, further subdivided into two half pennies, and four farthings (quarter pennies). Therefore, our 25 shillings equates to 300 pence, which converts to £300. It's not a perfect conversion, but I think it gives a better comparison.)

A Steep High Hill

Contents

The History of the village of Blue Bell Hill
A Steep High Hill

The Upper Bell Public House
Jillian Allonby ©1994

Chapter One
Highway to the South

The 20th century settlement of Blue Bell Hill developed along the main road from Rochester to Maidstone. Let us, therefore, start our history of Blue Bell Hill by considering this road. Present day commuters know it as a busy road, a congested road. It is also a very ancient route. The Roman road, from Rochester to the iron-producing areas of the Weald, ran down Blue Bell Hill, though not on the line of the modern main road. The route may be even older. Before the Romans came, there was an Iron Age settlement at Rochester, affluent enough to mint its own coinage. It is quite possible that iron was already being worked in the Weald and transported to Rochester along our road, and that the Romans merely took over and improved an existing track. Two coins, one bearing the head of Vesenius, and one of Eppilus, were found in 1836 on a site halfway down Warren Road. These two men were rulers of east Kent during the first half of the first century AD, just before the Roman conquest.[1]

The Roman Road from Rochester followed the line of Delce Road, St William's Way, the upper end of City Way, and the A229 from Horsted, past the airfield and the Crest Hotel to a point behind the former site of the Bridgewood Cottage, subsequently the Bridgewood Pub, which no longer exists. From here, it slanted along the little valley, now occupied by Toddington Crescent, crossed Robin Hood Lane, and ran in a straight line to the junction of Mill Lane and Warren Road, behind the Upper Bell. It passed down Warren Road, including the zigzag at the lower end, along the sunken track to Cossington Service Station, thence to Maidstone, where Week Street, Gabriel's Hill and Stone Street still follow the line laid down 2,000 years ago.[2]

During Jutish (Anglo-Saxon) and mediaeval times, upkeep of the King's Highway was the responsibility of the manors, until an Act of 1555 transferred it to the parishes, which were becoming more important as the manorial system declined. The pattern of our local parish boundaries reflects this early responsibility. Nowhere do the parish boundaries follow the Roman Road. They cross it in such a way as to divide it into lengths, each length lying wholly within a given parish. Burham parish had the length between Mill Lane and Bridgewood Cottage. Aylesford parish had two lengths, one to the north and one to the south of Burham's portion. I shall suggest an explanation of this in Chapter Six. The larger southern portion extended from Tyland to Mill Lane. The shorter, northern portion lay between the M2 and the boundary with Chatham, just north of the Bridgewood roundabout. The boundary stone has been moved to a position near Asda, where it is no longer on the boundary. (see *Map 1*).

The parish system of maintenance was neither satisfactory, nor popular. Every able-bodied man was required to work four days a year on road maintenance; in 1691, this was increased to six days. Anyone owning a cart could expect it to be commandeered four days a year. A Parish Surveyor was appointed, one of his duties being to ensure that every parishioner did his 'statute work', or provided an acceptable substitute or a money payment in commutation of his duty. Understandably, the post of Parish Surveyor was not popular. In passing, the dumping of litter on or beside the highway is not a modern problem — the Accounts of Aylesford Parish Surveyors[3.1] include such entries as:

Dec 15th 1810	2 men and 1 horse and cart moving rubbish 1 day	8/6
Feb 6th 1811	2 men and 2 horses 1 day carrying rubbish	14/6
Mar 2nd 1811	2 men and 2 horses 1 day removing rubbish in the Roman road	12/–

Increase in population, in trade and in wheeled traffic gradually rendered the parish system of maintenance inadequate, particularly on major routes which passed through a number of parishes. Consequently, in the 18th century, Turnpike Trusts arose to supplement the work of the parishes. Each Turnpike Trust was set up by Act of Parliament, and was granted the right to charge tolls on one or more specified roads, the money so raised to be spent on maintaining or improving the road or roads. The majority of Trusts were set up between 1750 and 1800, but the road down Blue Bell Hill was turnpiked at an early date (1728), being only the third road in the county to be turnpiked.[4]

The full title of the Act of 1728[5.1] was "An Act for Repairing and Enlarging the Road leading from the house called the Sign of the Bells in the Parish of St Margaret's in Rochester to Maidstone and other roads there-in mentioned in the County of Kent". The 'other roads' lay on the far side of Maidstone, leading towards Malling and Wrotham Heath, and need not concern us on Blue Bell Hill. With respect to

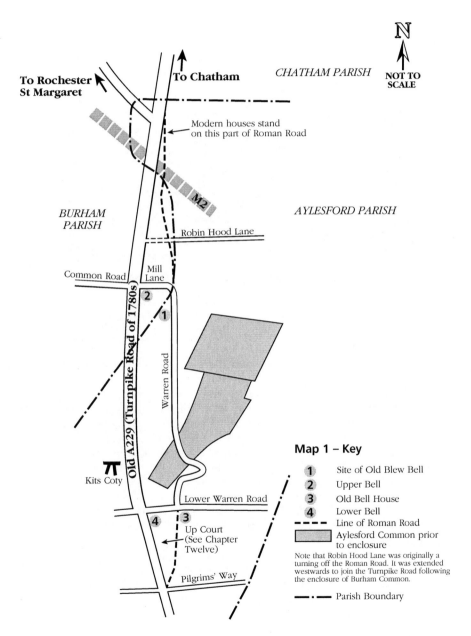

To Rochester
St Margaret

To Chatham

CHATHAM PARISH

N

NOT TO
SCALE

Modern houses stand
on this part of Roman Road

M2

BURHAM
PARISH

AYLESFORD PARISH

Robin Hood Lane

Common Road

Mill
Lane

Old A229 (Turnpike Road of 1780s)

2

1

Warren Road

Kits Coty

Lower Warren Road

4

3

Up Court
(See Chapter
Twelve)

Pilgrims' Way

Map 1 – Key

1 Site of Old Blew Bell
2 Upper Bell
3 Old Bell House
4 Lower Bell
- - - - Line of Roman Road
[ ] Aylesford Common prior
     to enclosure

Note that Robin Hood Lane was originally a
turning off the Roman Road. It was extended
westwards to join the Turnpike Road following
the enclosure of Burham Common.

— · — Parish Boundary

Plate 1   *Junction of Rochester Road (now the B2097) and Chatham Road
(A229) at Bridgewood, approximately 1930. The road to the left was
turnpiked in 1727, that to the right in 1821, hence the old name of this
junction as the Bridgewood Gates. The house was occupied earlier
in the 20th century by Mr and Mrs Whitbread (see Chapter Three).*
(Photograph courtesy of Mrs Madge Johnson.)

the Rochester–Maidstone Road, the Turnpike Trustees did not take
over the whole of the Roman Road, but only that portion of it which
lay between Maidstone and Bridgewood. Between Bridgewood and
Rochester they chose the Rochester–Maidstone Road (now the B2097)
(*Plate 1*). The Act gave the Trustees the right to charge tolls for 21
years "provided never-the-less that if at any time before the expiration
of the said term of 21 years the said road shall be sufficiently amended
and repaired and is so adjudged by the JPs … the toll or duty shall
cease". This was optimistic. It was to be 140 years before the tolls were
discontinued. It was during this 140 years that the Trustees diverted
the road away from the line laid down by the Romans to the route
which we know as the old A229, around which Blue Bell Hill Village
was to develop.

The Trustees did not have an easy task. Being only the third Turnpike Trust in the county, it was very much in the nature of a pilot
scheme, there being little expertise or experience to guide the Trustees.[3.6] They were given no funds. The ordinary people disliked paying
tolls and would sometimes go to considerable lengths to avoid doing

so. The parishes saw it as an opportunity to avoid doing their 'statute work', even though the Act stated that they were still responsible for it. The promoters of the Trust had probably underestimated the physical magnitude of the task. To add to their problems, the Act was badly worded, so that seven years and several court cases later, the Trustees had to apply for another Act of Parliament to "explain and amend" the first one.[5.2] The court cases, and the costs of obtaining the second Act, swallowed the income which should have been spent on maintaining the roads. Despite these setbacks, by the end of 21 years, the roads on the other side of Maidstone were much improved. The Rochester–Maidstone Road, however, was still unsatisfactory, so in 1749 the Trustees applied for an extension of time for another 21 years, again with the optimistic proviso that tolls would cease earlier if the road reached the required standard.[5.3]

They then soldiered on until 1773, when they sought an extension of both time and powers.[5.4] By now, the Trust had more than 40 years' experience, and its members were aware of the snags in the system. This shows clearly if the 1773 Act is compared with the original one of 1728. For example, the original Act laid down that any carriage drawn by four or more horses should pay a toll of 1/–. The 1773 Act laid down a toll of 3d per horse, thus ensuring that 8-horse teams (the HGVs of the 18th century) paid toll which was, quite literally, proportional to their horse-power. A new toll was included, stipulating that "every horse drawing in a carriage laden with timber between Nov 1st and April 1st" was to be charged at the double rate of 6d per horse. In addition, "If any person draws ... any tree or piece of timber ... other than upon a wheel carriage, or if any piece of timber on a wheel carriage drags in the road ... Penalty £2". Reading between the lines, and bearing in mind the extent of the woodlands on Blue Bell Hill, we begin to understand why, after 45 years, the road was still unsatisfactory.

The Act of 1773 was an extensive one, with important implications for Blue Bell Hill. In particular, it empowered the Trustees to "divert, turn, shorten, vary or alter the course of the road". Under the original Act, they were empowered only to widen the road, consequently this still followed the Roman line — including Warren Road, which, being sunken, was difficult to widen. All the wear and tear must have been concentrated into a very narrow strip. Judging from consequent events, the Trustees had decided that the only solution was a major diversion to cut out Warren Road. The 1773 Act enabled them to do this. However, life was never easy for the Trustees. The Act gave them extensive new powers and extended their existing powers for another

21 years, but only on condition that they repaid £800 which they had borrowed to carry out work at the Rochester end of the road. Thus, they now had the powers which they needed, but no money to implement them. Doubtless the Officers of KCC's Highways Department will sympathise!

The Trustees rose to the occasion. They contacted their colleagues of the Turnpike Trust which controlled the road from Dartford and Gravesend to Rochester. This Trust was senior to ours, having been in existence since 1712. There was some overlap of personnel. Together, the two sets of Trustees persuaded Parliament that it was in everyone's interests that road travel from London to Maidstone (via Gravesend and Rochester of course) should be encouraged. The terms of their petition are set out thus:

"... there is a very steep high hill upon the road between Rochester and Maidstone called Boxley Hill and it would be of great benefit to travellers if the course of the road was altered so as to avoid the said hill, and such alteration might induce many persons having occasion to travel between London and Maidstone, whereby the toll arising ... would be increased, but the [present] tolls are not sufficient to defray the expense of such alteration ... the Trustees of the [Gravesend] road are willing to allow £100 PA out of tolls towards defraying the expenses of altering the course of the road from Rochester to Maidstone ...", etc. The Act authorising this financial arrangement was passed in 1782.[5.5]

The Trustees now had both the powers and the money to divert the road. They wasted no time. An indenture of 1786[3.3] refers to the Bell House as having been "lately built". The original Bell House was near the top of Warren Road — or Boxley Hill, to use the 18th century name — just within Aylesford parish. When the road was shifted, the pub promptly went after it, thus moving into Burham parish. Another probable reference to the construction of the new road is Thorpe's comment, in 1788, about "digging down the banks, some years since, to enlarge and widen the great road near old Blue-bell Ale House which is situated just above Kits Coty House".[6] It is a reasonable deduction that the road was diverted between 1782 and 1786. The diversion was a major one. It left the line of the Roman Road at Cossington Service Station and rejoined it just south of Bridgewood Cottage. It included the length of road around which Blue Bell Hill Village would develop (*Plate 2*). It would see the advent of the internal combustion engine and double-decker buses, and would serve as a main road for 200 years. It was superseded in the 1970s and 1980s by the new A229, but still forms the north-bound slip-road from Cossington Service Station to the Lower

Chatham Road, Blue Bell Hill.

Plate 2   *Road through the northern part of the village, approaching Bridgewood Gates, approximately 1930. Note the very wide verge and the lack of street lighting. The houses at the right of the photograph stand on the line of the Roman Road. Pilcher's Garage and the junction with Hallfield Road are indicated by the group of cars. (Photograph courtesy of Mrs Madge Johnson.)*

Bell, and the south-bound slip-road from the Upper Bell. Two other lengths survive as Old Chatham Road, providing access to Lower Bell Industries and Kits Coty Restaurant, and the cul-de-sac north of Salisbury Road, which forms part of the pedestrian route up the hill.

By 1801, the Trustees were erecting additional gates where side-roads joined the main road. In the Aylesford Vestry Meeting Minutes for 1801 it is recorded that:

"It was resolved in consideration that the Parish of Aylesford have it in contemplation to improve the road in that parish leading from Aylesford ... to Kits Coty House and from thence up Great Down Field and to join on the Common to Rochester Road and of the expense they will be put to by such improvement the following Trustees were of the opinion that a Side-Bar ought not to be put up on that Cross-road."[3.2]

There is then a recorded vote, listing those Trustees who voted against a side-bar. There is no record of those voting in favour of it, so we do not know whether the proposal was carried out or not. The Ordnance Survey map of 1819 shows Turnpikes at Bridgewood and at Brick-on-Edge Cottage (where the Pilgrims' Way crosses the Roman Road) but not between these two, but neither does it show a Turnpike

7

at Sandling, where a gate existed from 1728 onwards. There is an entry in the Accounts of the Parish Surveyors, dated 11th October 1811, which reads: "Paid John Baker for opening the water tables on both sides of the road from the stream to Kits Cot House Gate … £19–2–0d." which may indicate that the side-bar was erected.

The cross-road referred to is probably the junction by the Lower Bell. Mention of the Common suggests that the course of the diverted road was influenced by a provision of the 1773 Act, that if the line of the new road lay on common land the Trustees did not have to compensate the owner. It may explain why, from the Lower Bell, the new road went uphill rather steeply along the road we know as Old Chatham Road. This lay on the Common. An indenture of 1813 refers to two pieces of land, totalling just over two acres (0.8ha), "… taken off and enclosed … from Aylesford Common adjacent the new road leading from Maidstone to Rochester."[3.4] Six years later there is another reference to these enclosures, but now referring to "that new-erected brick-built messuage or tenement, stables and premises there-to belonging commonly known by the name and sign of Kits Coty House" built on the enclosed land.[3.5] These indentures also indicate the extent of Aylesford Common, referred to again in Chapter Two.

The last important Turnpike Act affecting Blue Bell Hill was passed in 1821.[5.6] It authorised the Trustees to take over the road from Bridgewood to Chatham. There was already a gate at Bridgewood controlling the road to Rochester, but with the growth of Chatham as a dockyard and military town during the 18th century, traffic along the Chatham Road was increasing. Smith[7] states that by 1836 there was an extensive local coach service based in Maidstone, serving Chatham and Brompton. The hey-day of the coaches was the period from 1820–1840, but the military connection with Chatham may have given rise to an earlier increase, particularly during the Napoleonic Wars.

The Act of 1821 empowered the Trustees to divert the road as well as turnpike it. This diversion was probably intended to straighten the road. The earlier diversion of the 1780s had created the present road through the village, but at its northern end, this rejoined the Roman Road, which, it will be remembered, lay further east, running up the little valley where Toddington Crescent now stands. North of the M2 its line is represented by the houses on the east of the A229, which literally stand on the Roman Road. The join between the 1780s Turnpike Road and the Roman Road must have created a very sharp bend, which may well have become an early accident black-spot. We can imagine the young 'bloods' from Maidstone barracks getting up a good speed on horseback or carriage as they started the long downward slope from the Upper Bell, only to meet this unexpected kink in the road. Under the 1821 Act, the Trustees eliminated the kink, continuing the road northwards in a straight line past where the Bridgewood Cottage, Bridgewood House and Baptist Chapel would later be built. It is, perhaps, ironic that 140 years later the Ministry of Transport should reinstate the kink when they built Taddington Wood roundabout to serve the link roads on to the M2. (The roundabout and link roads subsequently disappeared when the M2 was widened in the early 2000s.)

The straightening was continued northwards until the new diversion merged imperceptibly in the Roman Road, somewhere in the vicinity of the Crest Hotel. Until about 1950, the Roman Road was visible as a raised mound and ditch running through the front gardens of the houses on the east side of the road, north of the boundary with Chatham.[2] The gardens, which were unusually long, were shortened to provide land for dualling this stretch of road, and the last vestiges of the Roman Road disappeared.

The Trustees were by now in some financial difficulty. They owed a total of £4,950.[5,6] They considered that it would be "of great benefit ... and public utility if the Chatham Road were turnpiked and improved", but they also recognised that the tolls from the Bridgewood Gates would be "found insufficient". Consequently, the Act repealed the normal tolls payable at these gates, and replaced them with greater ones. Thus, the toll for every horse, mule, ass or other beast drawing in a cart increased from 3d to 4½d, cattle increased from 10d per score to 1s 3d per score, and the charge for horses or other beasts drawing timber during the winter increased from 6d per animal to 9d. As usual, the Act authorised the Trustees to charge tolls for 21 years, but they seem to have continued for twice this length of time. Not until 1st November 1867 did the first of the Annual Turnpike Acts release the Trustees from their 140-years-old commitment; it was an indication of the importance of our road, even then, that it was included in the first batch of roads to be taken over by the newly-constituted Highway Boards. In a final fling, possibly to reduce their debts, the Trustees sold off property which was surplus to requirement. In a terrier of the Rochester Bridge Wardens[8] there is reference to a cottage erected "near the site of the old Bridgewood Toll House purchased in 1867 of the Trustees of the Rochester and Maidstone Turnpike Road with garden, occupied by the Woodreve, rent free." Further on in the same terrier, we find a note: "By a conveyance dated 5/10/67 the Trustees of the Maidstone and Rochester Turnpike Trust conveyed to the Wardens all their rights in the slips of roads contiguous to the East and West sides of the road between the Toll House and Rochester". The KCC Highways Surveyors may wish that they still owned these slips for road widening purposes!

Thus did the Surveyors and Engineers of the Imperial Roman Empire and the Trustees of the Rochester–Maidstone Turnpike Road set the scene for the development of a 20th century village.

Highway to the South

1) Kelly, D B, **Quarry Wood Camp, Loose: A Belgic Oppidum**, *Archeologia Cantania* Vol 86, p 74.

2) Margary, I D, **Roman Roads in the Weald**, 1948.

3) **Kent Archives Office** — sundry documents.

    3.1) P12/21/1 Accounts of the Aylesford Parish Surveyors, 1810–1849

    3.2) P12/8/1 Aylesford Vestry Minutes

    3.3) U 896/T5 Indenture of Lease & Release, November 13th 1786

    3.4) U 896/T1 Indenture of Lease & Release, May 14th 1813

    3.5) U 896/T1 Indenture of Lease & Release, June 1st 1819

    3.6) T12/1 Minutes of the Rochester–Maidstone Turnpike Trust, 1728–1741

4) Jessup, F W, **Kent History Illustrated**, p 48.

5) Turnpike Acts relating to the Rochester–Maidstone Road.

    5.1) 1728 (1 George II), Springfield Local History Library

    5.2) 1736 (9 George II) PG Cap 7, Springfield Local History Library

    5.3) 1749 (22 George II) PG Cap 8, Springfield Local History Library

    5.4) 1773 (13 George III) PG Cap 114, House of Lords Record Office

    5.5) 1782 (22 George III) PG Cap 98, House of Lords Record Office

    5.6) 1821 (1 & 2 George IV) L & P Cap x, House of Lords Record Office

    5.7) 1867 (30 & 31 Victoria) RG Cap 121, House of Lords Record Office

6) Thorpe, J, **Custumale Roffense** (1788).

7) Smith, T P, **Geographical Pattern of Coaching Services in Kent, 1836**. *Archeologia Cantania* XCVIII, 1982, p 191 onwards.

8) Terrier of the Rochester Bridge Wardens.

Chapter Two
The Commons

At the beginning of the 19th century there were still 500 acres (202ha) of common land in the three parishes of Burham, Aylesford and Wouldham. Some of it was common pasture by the river, but most of it lay on the great sweep of downland from Wouldham to the Lower Bell. Piecemeal enclosure had already occurred and by the end of the century, all three commons would be enclosed by Act of Parliament. Of the three, Burham Common was the most important for the development of Blue Bell Hill village. It still comprised about 300 acres (121ha), extending on both sides of Common Road and stretching from the boundary with Wouldham to Robin Hood Lane and Podkin Meadow; both the Roman Road and the new Turnpike Road lay on it. It thus included most of the land on which the village now stands. Until it was enclosed, no village could develop.

Although it was the earliest of the three to be enclosed, the Act being passed in 1812 and the Award completed in 1815,[1.1] it is the common for which the sense of 'belonging to the people' (which common land never did anyway!) has remained the strongest. This may be because the name Common Road has maintained the tradition. It may be because the superb view from the downs makes it a natural honey-pot area. It may be because the residents of Blue Bell Hill have quietly, but firmly, declined to accept that the Common is not theirs. Thus, in September 1929, we find Blue Bell Hill Rate-payers' Association minuting, under a heading 'Burham Downs', that "The Hon. Secretary called attention to the fact that the Sub-tenant was preventing persons from picnicking on the Hill ... It was unanimously agreed that Mr Burman the Tenant be approached with regards to safe-guarding the public interests". [2] This resolution loftily ignored the little detail that the public no longer had any rights over the land.

The instigator of the enclosure seems to have been one Mr Summerfield, the Earl of Aylesford's estate manager.[1.2] In 1805 we find him reporting that "The rights of soil belong to your Lordship. This

Common ... contains upwards of 300 acres [121ha], almost entirely covered over with scrub oaks and brambles. Sheep and cattle are pastured in the summer but there is little feed and the distance is so far from them who have the right of common that very small advantage is derived from it. The Farmers and Cottagers have the privilege of cutting bushes but from the great length of carriage hardly think it worth their while; indeed in its present rude state it is unprofitable to all parties. The soil is not of a bad quality and if cleared I have no doubt might be converted into good corn land ... ."

The Common seems to have deteriorated during the 100 years since 1706, when an indenture of sale of Great Culand listed the right of common pasturage for 200 sheep with other assets of the farm.[1.3] Mr Summerfield's mention of corn land probably reflects the fact that, when he was writing, England was at war and subject to blockade which made it difficult to import food. 1805 was the year of the Battle of Trafalgar, in which Nelson died, reputedly in the arms of Purser Burke lived at Wouldham. 1815, when the Enclosure Award was completed, was the year of the Battle of Waterloo, which saw the final defeat and eclipse of Napoleon. Nationally, the Napoleonic Wars were a peak period of enclosure of common land.

Mr Summerfield may have been correct in saying that the Commoners, which included all the free-holders of the parish, hardly thought it worth their while to exercise their common rights, but when there was a possibility of obtaining an extra bit of freehold land in compensation for those rights, they thought it very much worth their while. The abstract of claims for compensation included no fewer than 28 claimants.[1.1] The Earl wanted his manorial allotment, the Rector wanted tithes, Burham parish wanted land for their poor and, unexpectedly, so did the Churchwardens of Chatham. Everyone else wanted whatever they could get. Even the Wardens of Rochester Bridge joined in. They owned five acres (2ha) of pasture near the river, out of total holdings in North Kent amounting to 2,000 acres (809ha). In the event, they were allocated 3 rods, 16 perches (just over three-quarters of an acre, a third of a hectare), which they promptly leased to the Earl of Aylesford for 5/– a year. This arrangement still appertained in 1921, being recorded in a terrier of the Bridge Lands for that year.

Behind the claim of the Churchwardens of Chatham lies a 'near miss' in the previous century. A Commissioner of H M Dockyard, Sir Edmund Gregory, by his will dated 24th April 1710, bequeathed £100 to the Minister and Churchwardens of Chatham, the interest to be distributed annually amongst the poor of Chatham.[3] This money was invested in

South Sea Stock, which was sold in 1720 for £750. The Churchwardens were lucky: 1720 was the year of the early stock market crash, known to history as the bursting of the South Sea Bubble. The Churchwardens must have sold out just in time. They used the money to buy Pett's Farm in Burham, which they still held when the Common was enclosed. The farm and the land which they obtained under the Enclosure Award were, in 1828, leased out at £31 per year "which is stated to be a good rent". They did better out of the Enclosure Award than Burham itself. Petts' Farm consisted of 27 acres (11ha), for which they received five acres (2ha) under the award. The Overseers of the Poor of Burham, with seven acres under their control, received only half an acre (0.2ha). This was situated near the east end of Common Road. Most of the house plots along Common Road had their origin in the Enclosure Award of 1815, being little parcels of land allocated to small-holders in the parish as compensation for their loss of common rights.[1.1]

To defray the expenses of "carrying the Act into execution", the Commissioners decided to sell 38 acres (15.3ha) by public auction, held at Kits Coty House on April 25th 1812.[4] The area chosen for auction was the triangle bounded by Mill Lane, the new Turnpike Road and the Roman Road. The auction raised £730, giving an average of £19 per acre. One large plot, lying west of the main road, was also sold, being bought by the Earl of Aylesford for £375. It was this land, together with adjacent plots, which he bought at a second auction, which became known as Lord Lees. Whether the auction was insufficient to cover all expenses or whether there was pressure to make some of the land more widely available is not indicated in the award, but a year later there was a second auction. This time, all lots lay west of the main road. Bidding seems to have been less brisk than at the first auction. Two lots did not reach their reserve prices, and were withdrawn by the Commissioners, being sold subsequently by private contract. The Earl of Aylesford bought three lots, adjacent to each other and to his earlier purchase. Eight acres fronting onto Common Road were bought by John Boys, a builder from Teston. He was somewhat ahead of his time. It was to be another 100 years before development became more than sporadic.

The Enclosure Award set out the roads which were to serve the new pattern of land-holdings. All the time the land was common — 1,000 years or more — people could pass freely across it any direction. Once it was enclosed, this would no longer be possible. The long years of use had resulted in a number of clearly-defined routes, some of which converged on the Robin Hood pub. These were drift, or drove

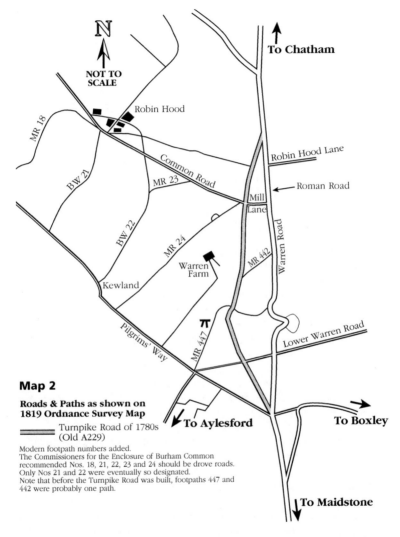

N

NOT TO
SCALE

To Chatham

Robin Hood

MR 18

Robin Hood Lane

Common Road

BW 21

Roman Road

MR 23

Mill
Lane

BW 22

MR 24

Warren Road

MR 442

Warren
Farm

Kewland

π

Pilgrims' Way

MR 447

Lower Warren Road

Map 2

**Roads & Paths as shown on
1819 Ordnance Survey Map**

Turnpike Road of 1780s
(Old A229)

↙**To Aylesford**

→
To Boxley

Modern footpath numbers added.
The Commissioners for the Enclosure of Burham Common
recommended Nos. 18, 21, 22, 23 and 24 should be drove roads.
Only Nos 21 and 22 were eventually so designated.
Note that before the Turnpike Road was built, footpaths 447 and
442 were probably one path.

↓**To Maidstone**

roads, along which cattle were herded onto the Common, past the pub, down into Nashenden Valley and up the other side and hence to Rochester market. The Commissioners proposed that eight routes be designated as 'carriage-roads or drift roads',[5] but they arranged for objections to be made and a public enquiry to be held, and in the event, only five of the routes were designated.[1.1] Common Road, Mill Lane and the upper end of Robin Hood Lane became carriage-roads. Two of the tracks down the hill remained as drift-roads. These were the track which starts opposite the Robin Hood and runs straight down the hill to Burham village, and that which starts just west of 'Fairview' and slants south-eastwards to Culand. The status accorded them in the Enclosure Award explains why, on the modern Definitive Map of Foot-paths, these two tracks are shown as By-ways open to All Traffic. The three tracks which did not make the grade are still public rights-of-way, being shown on the Definitive Map as footpaths. They comprise FP18, at the far end of Common Road almost on the Wouldham boundary, FP23 at the western edge of the KCC Picnic Site, and FP24 which is the deeply-sunken path leading to the track between the two Culand pits and past the site of Great Culand (see *Map 2*).

The Commissioners stipulated that all Enclosure Award roads should be 30ft wide (9m), though some seem to have shrunk during the intervening period. Mill Lane and Common Road must have been one continuous track until severed by the new Turnpike Road. Common Road is referred to in the Enclosure Award as the Upper Green Way, a term which, like Drift and Drove Road, indicates a road along which cattle were driven, but may also indicate a very ancient road (see also Chapter Nine). The upper end of Robin Hood Lane was included to connect the lane with the new Turnpike Road. It was originally a turning off the Roman Road, approximately where the Village Hall now stands (see *Map 2*). When the Turnpike Trustees shifted the main road westwards, they left a gap between the lane and the new road. This did not matter all the time the surrounding area was common land, but once the common was enclosed people would not be able to walk across it. The Enclosure Commissioners therefore stipulated that a carriage or drift road, 30ft wide (9m), should "branch from the new turnpike road and cross the common in an easterly direction till it joins the present road leading to Ligeon". This late origin may explain why the top of the lane is prone to pot-holes. Unlike the rest of it, which has been consolidated by centuries of use, the length between the Village Hall and the main road originated as a go-as-you-please across The Common (*Plate 3*). 'Ligeon' I interpret as Lidging. This was the old pronunciation of Lidsing, which was of greater importance in past centuries than today. The 1819 Ordnance Survey map shows a track continuing the line of Robin Hood Lane along the northern edge of The Common, parallel with Common Road, to the 'Robin Hood' pub, but the Commissioners did not include this track in their proposals.

Robin Hood Lane, near Upper Bell

Plate 3   *Upper end of Robin Hood Lane, approaching the junction with the
Maidstone/Chatham road, approximately 1930. This was the 'missing
link' which connected the lane to the Turnpike Road of the 1780s; the
land on either side was originally common land until it was enclosed
in 1815. The Roman Road ran where Toddington Crescent now lies;
there is a curious mark on the road in the middle of the photograph
which may indicate the position of the Roman Road.*
(Photograph courtesy of Mrs Madge Johnson.)

Indeed, they referred to it as a private road, though part of the modern
FP14 follows its line.

The second of the three commons to be enclosed was Aylesford's.
The Tithe Map of 1841 shows 32 acres (13ha) of common land,[14] some
lying east of Warren Road where Hazelwood Farm now stands, and
some extending westwards down the hill to the old A229, and the path
by Kits Coty (the megalith). We have already seen, in Chapter One, that
Kits Coty House (the modern restaurant) was built on land enclosed
from the Common. The pattern of land-holdings in this area, as shown
on the Tithe Map and Assessment, suggests that the whole shoulder
of downland above the 'Lower Bell' was once common land. The
great bank which towered above the old A229, now cut away to make
room for the new A229, was called Common Waste Hill. By the time
of the final enclosure in 1854, the Common had shrunk still further to
24 acres (9.7ha)[15] (see *Map 3*).

On Burham Common, as on many others, the Commoners exer-

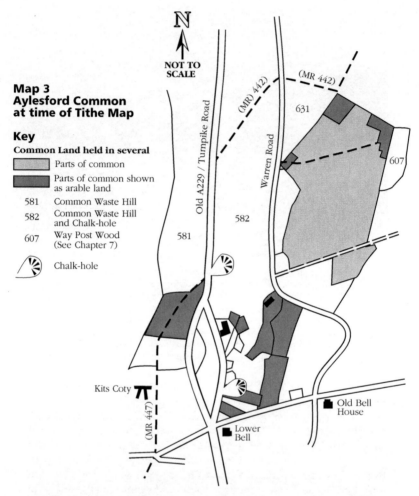

**Map 3
Aylesford Common
at time of Tithe Map**

Key

Common Land held in several

Parts of common

Parts of common shown as arable land

581   Common Waste Hill

582   Common Waste Hill and Chalk-hole

607   Way Post Wood (See Chapter 7)

Chalk-hole

N

NOT TO SCALE

(MR 442)

(MR 442)

631

607

Old A229 / Turnpike Road

Warren Road

582

581

Kits Coty

(MR 447)

Old Bell House

Lower Bell

cised their rights over the whole common. These rights usually included pasturing of sheep or cattle, the number of animals which each Commoner was entitled to graze being regulated by the manorial courts. Other rights were often included, such as collecting wood or bushes for fencing, or bracken for bedding. This arrangement may have applied on Aylesford Common in earlier times, but the Tithe Map shows that, by 1841, what was left of it was held 'in several'. That is, it was divided into discrete parcels of land each occupied by a named individual. Some of the parcels were cultivated as arable land. Under the Enclosure Award none of the occupiers of these parcels of land was granted an allotment in compensation for loss of common rights, since none of them was a free-holder of the parish. Allotments were granted in respect of some of the woods on the Hill (Taddington and the woods of Robin Hood Farm). In addition to agricultural use, Aylesford parish used its common for road repairs. Thus, in March 1812, the Parish Surveyors paid John Florry 9/– for cutting 150 faggots on the Common to put in the roads,[1.6] an entry which suggests that it was in no better condition than Burham Common at the same time. The Surveyors were permitted to take material from common land for the repair of roads, a facility which was extended to the Turnpike Trustees also.

Wouldham was the last of the three parishes to lose its common land. The Act was passed in 1862, and the award completed in 1866.[1.7] The total area was 163 acres (66ha), of which about 30 acres (12ha) was common grazing on the saltings near the old ferry. By this time, the importance of common land for recreation was being recognised. It was in 1865 that the Commons Preservation Society was set up,[6] many of the founder members being themselves wealthy commoners. The activities of the Society saved such areas of common land as Hampstead Heath, Wimbledon Common and Epping Forest for the enjoyment of future Londoners, and paved the way for the preservation of commons outside London, such as (in Kent) Dartford Heath, and the commons around Tunbridge Wells, to say nothing of a multitude of village greens, such as those at Boxley, Bearsted and West Peckham. Consequently, when Wouldham Common was enclosed, four acres were allocated to the parish for recreational purposes; this little common of four acres is still the property of Wouldham Parish Council. Walkers along Common Road and the North Downs Way to Lower Nashenden may have seen it on the south side of the track. Guard it well, Wouldham. It is all that remains of the great swathe of land along which, 1,000 years ago, the community walked at will along the brow of our downs.

The Commons

1)   Kent Archives Office.
   1.1)   Q/RDC/3 A-C Enclosure Award, Burham Common.
   1.2)   U 234 E21 Earl of Aylesford's Estate Papers.
   1.3)   U 234 T17 Indenture of sale, Great Culand, 1706.
   1.4)   CTR 12 B Aylesford Tithe Map.
       CTR 12 A Aylesford Tithe Assessment.
   1.5)   Q/RDC/19 Enclosure Award, Aylesford Common.
   1.6)   P/12/21/1 Accounts of Highways Surveyor of Aylesford Parish, 1810-1849.
   1.7)   Q/RDC/25 Enclosure Award, Wouldham Common.
2)   Minutes of the Blue Bell Hill Rate-payers' Association, 1929–1947 (unpublished material).
3)   Report of the Charity Commissioners, 1832–1837.
4)   *Maidstone Journal and Kentish Advertiser*, April 14th 1812 (Public notice of auction). Available on micro-film, Maidstone Library.
5)   *Maidstone Journal and Kentish Advertiser*, May 5th 1812 (Public notice of roads to be retained after enclosure).
6)   Williams, W.H., OBE, MA, LLB., **The Commons, Open Spaces and Footpaths Preservation Society, 1865–1965**.

Chapter Three
The Village Develops
1820–1920

By 1820, the scene was set for the development of the village. The Turnpike Road had been in existence for 30 years and the Turnpike Trust was about to take over responsibility for the road to Chatham. Stage coaches were running from Maidstone to Chatham, Brompton and Rochester. 'The Old Blew Bell', at the top of Warren Road, had been replaced by the 'Upper Bell', in its present position. Burham Common had been enclosed and the Enclosure Award ensured that Mill Lane, Common Road and the 'missing link' at the top of Robin Hood Lane were public roads. Despite this, development during the rest of the 19th century was slow and scattered. One possible explanation is lack of employment. The chalk-pits did not yet exist and, in an age dominated by agriculture, there was little farmland. The extensive woodlands, which reached in one direction down Nashenden Valley, and in the other to Walderslade Bottom and beyond, provided limited employment which could not be expanded to accommodate a larger population.

In 1820, there was a scatter of houses near the 'Upper Bell', including 'The Old Blew Bell', and two tenements adjacent the fields behind the Crematorium. At the far end of Common Road were 'The Robin Hood' pub, Costin's Farm (now Hill Farm) and a group of cottages associated with them. A Turnpike Cottage stood at the Bridgewood Gates. By 1842, the number had crept up.[1] The group by the 'Upper Bell' had increased slightly. The mill, which gave Mill Lane its name, was built. It was a typical Kentish smock mill, used to grind corn, with an octagonal base.[2] It would remain until 1890, when it was 'tail-winded' in a gale.[15] Along Common Road houses had been built on some of the allotments granted to small land-owners in the Enclosure Award. Of the larger houses, the Bridgewood Cottage and Bridgewood House adjacent to it were both built, the former being an ale-house (*Plates 4* and *5*). They were owned by Carter Bye, who also owned the field along Common Road, which is now the Sports Field. It is not clear whether 'Carter' was his first name or his trade; tithe assessments did not usually record an individual's trade. Just south of where the telephone exchange now stands, was the large house, later called 'Woodside'. In

Plate 4   *Bridgewood House. This was probably built between 1821, when the road through the village was straightened by the Turnpike Trust (see Chapter One), and 1842, when the house was shown on Burham Tithe Map. For most of the 20th century it was occupied by the Barling family. The building has now been demolished.*

1842, it was owned and occupied by T H Hooper, Esq. From the number of outbuildings, it could have been a farm, but the only land held by him was three acres of pasture attached to the house. In the Register of Electors for 1868–1869, Mr E T Hooper qualified as an elector in the Mid-Kent Division by virtue of owning a free-hold house and land on Blue Bell Hill, though his address was in Bayswater.[3] This suggests that the first Mr Hooper built the house as a country residence, as envisaged by the Enclosure Commissioners. Their advertisement of the auction held in 1812 (see Reference 4 of Chapter Two) suggested that it offered "an unprecedented opportunity to any person wishing to purchase a situation in the country possessing every advantage of health and convenience … within 4 miles [6.4km] of Rochester or Maidstone and 32 [51.5km] from London; adjoining the Turnpike Road where stage coaches and other carriages are passing every hour …". Facing 'Woodside', across the road, where the entrance to Laurie Grey Avenue now lies, stood 2–4 small tenements.

    Further from the centre of the future village, Kits Coty House was built by 1812, when the first auction of common land was held in it. The 'Lower

Plate 5   'The Bridgewood Cottage', more familiarly known as the
           Bridgewood Pub. It stood next to Bridgewood House, and its front
           view was similar to its neighbour, but...

Plate 6   ...much of its northern wall was constructed of flint-work,
           suggesting that it may have had an older origin. The building has
           now been demolished.

Plate 7   *Blue Bell Hill Chapel in 1987. Alterations to the road layout associated with the construction of the original M2, and later of the village by-pass, isolated the chapel in a* cul-de-sac, *which was not easily accessible. Development in the Walderslade/Lordswood area moved the centre of population away from Blue Bell Hill Village. The building has now been demolished.*   *(Photograph courtesy of Mrs J Howard.)*

Bell' was certainly built by 1828, when Shepherd's well-known sketch of the megalith shows in the background Kits Coty House, with its chimneys smoking merrily, and the 'Lower Bell' peeping coyly around the shoulder of the hill. It may have been built considerably earlier: like the 'Upper Bell', it may have shifted westwards as soon as the road was diverted.

Warren Farm itself was an older establishment. The Aylesford Tithe Map of 1841 shows buildings on the south side of the road, but all that remains of them now are the small shed and the mounting block at the far end of the road. An indenture of 1845 quotes an earlier one of 1805, which lists several generations of occupiers.[5] It was formerly in the tenure or occupation of "George Chowling, afterward of Edward Duke, since of Henry Fletcher, after that of Elizabeth Taylor, widow, then late of Edward Fowle deceased and then of George Fowle". A survey of the boundaries of Boxley parish taken in 1609,[6] refers to Sir Edward Duke. He lived at Great Cossington, near Aylesford village, and owned land in the vicinity of Cossington Fields Farm. The indenture of 1805, quoted above, indicates that he also owned Warren Farm, suggesting that his land-holding was continuous from Great Cossington to Cossington Fields, hence the name of the latter. (For those unfamiliar with the area, Cossington Fields Farm lies at the top of the downs, adjacent the M2, by the radio and television masts.) Cossington Fields Farmhouse is shown on the Boxley Tithe Map of 1849; Mr Merritt, who lived there for many years, told me that it was built in 1828. He also said that there were two old cottages, about where the wireless masts now stand; the former were later burnt down. He was told this by an old man who had once lived in one of them. The two old cottages were in Aylesford parish; William Balston, the Maidstone paper maker whose wife, Catherine, owned Cossington Field Farm, built the present house a few yards across the boundary, in Boxley parish. In passing, it is curious how many farms lie at the parish boundaries. In addition to Cossington Fields, there are Kits Coty Farm, Tyland Farm, Robin Hood House, and Scarborough. We are left wondering whether there was some advantage in locating them on the boundaries or whether the sites were already occupied when the boundaries were drawn up and, if so, how ancient these settlements are.

By 1864 the lime-works on Blue Bell Hill was well established, and the Ordnance Survey map of that year shows a group of cottages along Warren Road, on the brow of the hill above the lime-works, which accommodated the workers. Like the houses along Common Road, they were built on enclosed common land — this time Aylesford Common. Mr Sandford, whose family have owned the lime-works for 150 years, told me that the cottage nearest Warren Road was reputed to been a pub called the 'Holly Bush'. It also functioned as a school — whether simultaneously he was not certain! The houses were not well built. When the last one (Woodbine Villa!) was demolished in 1978, it was found to be built, not of chalk blocks, but of chalk slabs with rubble in between.

In 1892, Blue Bell Hill acquired a chapel (*Plates* 7 and *8*). Its two foundation stones inform us that:

THIS STONE WAS LAID	THIS STONE WAS LAID
BY	BY
COUNLLR. R.D. BATCHELOR	ALDN. F.F. BELSEY, J.P.
OCT. XII MDCCCXCII	OCT. XII MDCCCXCII

For fifteen years prior to this, Zion Baptist Church in Chatham had arranged afternoon Sunday School and Evening Service at Blue Bell Hill, the meetings being held in a wayside cottage kept by Mrs Green.[8] By the good offices of Alderman F F Belsey, who also subscribed £25

Plate 8   *Foundation Stone, Bluebell Hill Chapel. This was on the right of the door as you entered; in later years it was rather obscured by the porch which had been added. The other was on the left of the door and remained more conspicuous. Note the decorative line of flints, which extended around the whole building (see Chapter Eight). The building has now been demolished.*

to the building fund, and Mr A J Rogers, a plot of land was eventually obtained. It was typical of Blue Bell Hill's position in the no-man's land between Chatham and Maidstone that, although most of the houses lay in Burham and Aylesford parishes, its first place of worship was provided under the auspices of Chatham Chapel. The building was designed by Mr Denson, a member of Zion's congregation, and the stone-laying ceremony was conducted by Rev W W Brookside, from New Brompton. After the ceremony, they all repaired to the parent chapel in Clover Street, and had tea in the school-room, followed by celebratory speeches and a short concert. Councillor Burrell undertook to provide a free tea to the children on Blue Bell Hill — the village's first Sunday School treat.

At the ceremony it was noted that there was no religious accommodation of any kind within several miles of Blue Bell Hill. For 40 years, the Chapel was to remain the only place of worship in the developing village: in its heyday from 1892–1920, the congregation came from as far afield as Walderslade village, and the settlement around the 'Hook and Hatchet' (now 'The Poacher's Pocket'). Its faithful serv-

Plate 9   *Wooden house, dating from the first decade of the 20th century, possibly erected by Mr Brake. This type of house was common in the area. On the outside, there was a half-verandah and a square bay window; inside were four good-sized rooms, and, at the back, a small scullery. The one illustrated has now been destroyed, but a number of them were still in use in 1995.*   *(Photograph courtesy of Mrs J Howard.)*

ants included Mr Mills, who walked up the downs from Burham every Sunday to conduct the services, and Jack Trigg from Common Road, who for many years acted as caretaker and Sunday School Supervisor. Mr and Mrs Whitbread were also very active. He preached, she played the organ. This was not a pipe organ, but one of the little American Organs (sometimes called, incorrectly, harmoniums) which did such sterling service in a multitude of Mission Churches and household parlours. The Whitbreads lived in the old Toll Cottage at the Bridge-wood Gates, and every year organised a Sunday School Treat in the field where St Alban's Church now stands.[9]

Sunday Service was at that time a focus of social activity. Many a courtship originated in the invitation after service, 'Coming for a walk?' on the downs, or through the spring woods in which wood anemones, primroses, violets, early orchids, woodruff, wood sorrel and a host of

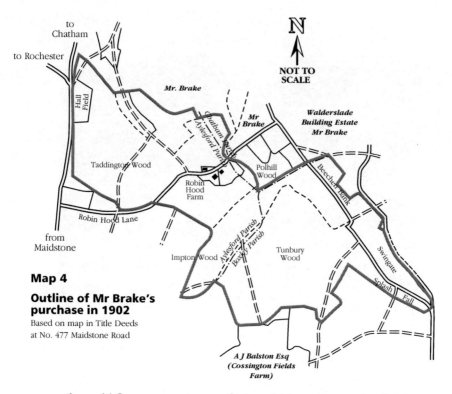

N

NOT TO
SCALE

to Chatham

to Rochester

Mr. Brake

Hall Field

Mr Brake

Chatham Parish
Aylesford Parish

Walderslade
Building Estate
Mr Brake

Taddington Wood

Polhill Wood

Beechen bank

Robin Hood Farm

Robin Hood Lane

from Maidstone

Aylesford Parish
Boxley Parish

Impton Wood

Tunbury Wood

Swingate

Splash Fall

Map 4

**Outline of Mr Brake's
purchase in 1902**

Based on map in Title Deeds
at No. 477 Maidstone Road

*A J Balston Esq
(Cossington Fields
Farm)*

other wild flowers grew in a profusion which young people of today
have never known. Even as late as the 1930s it was possible to pick
bunches of Lady Orchid at the edges of the woods. It was customary
at Easter for every window-sill of every church and chapel to be decorated along its whole length with primroses and violets picked from
the woods. The old Chapel served the developing village well, but
even as I write, its death knell sounds. In the *Kent Messenger* of 10th
March 1989, is the public notice that "The Registrar General, being
satisfied that Zion Gospel Mission Hall, Blue Bell Hill, Burham ... has
wholly ceased to be used as a place of worship by the congregation on
whose behalf it was on 10th March 1893 certified in accordance with
the Places of Worship Registration Act 1855, has cancelled the certifica-
tion". The old chapel served the developing village well, but has now
been demolished.

With the 20th century came land speculators. The woods east of
the A229 had, for nearly 200 years, been owned by the Best family.

Plate 10   A smaller type of wooden house, also found from the beginning of the
            20th century. The whole house was often covered in corrugated iron.

Plate 11   Mr and Mrs Stanley outside their house in Robin Hood Lane,
            approximately 1992. Houses of this design were common in the area
            before 1939. Some were built by Mr Brake, though the one in the
            photograph was built by Mr Stanley's father about 1920.

In 1901, they sold the land. 508 acres (205ha) were purchased by Mr H J E Brake, Auctioneer and Estate Agent from Farnborough, Hampshire, on behalf of Mr W H Brake of Walderslade. The extent of the purchase is shown on *Map 4*. Mr W H Brake was a land speculator rather than a developer, though he did offer to build houses for purchasers if they so wished. He advertised his land as suitable for a wide range of uses — one is tempted to say, for any use he could think of.[10] He offered prime residential sites and also small plots for artisan's houses. A small plot was 20ft x 200ft (6m x 60m), and sold for £10. Poultry farming, fruit growing, market gardening and investment in the existing chestnut coppice were other suggested uses. Of the pre-1939 houses in the area, two or three styles were common in the 1930s. Two of these are shown in *Plates 9* and *10*. The larger of these was probably the type erected by Mr Brake. Although built of wood, they should not be thought of as shacks. They were soundly built and well-designed for their time. A few are still in use, over 70 years later (*Plates 10* and *11*).

The building plots fronted onto the roads. At the time of purchase, only two roads were available to Mr Brake. Robin Hood Lane ran through his purchase. At the northern end of the village, near the Bridgewood Gates, some of his land fronted onto the main road. In order to offer more housing plots he laid out additional roads. Most of these were further east, near Robin Hood House, and adjacent Mr Brake's existing holdings in Walderslade, but two of them — Hallsfield and Victoria Road — impinged directly on the developing Blue Bell Hill village. The original Hall Field — spelt without an 's' — was a nine-acre (3.6ha) rectangular field, lying east of the main road. Mr Brake staked out Hallsfield Road around its northern and eastern edges. It had been cultivated since at least 1819, when the Ordnance Survey map shows it as one of the few parcels of land which was not wooded. Consequently, it needed little clearing before building could take place, and as the north end of the road was level and close to the main road, it developed as a residential road. The name probably comes from *hale*, meaning corner, being situated in the extreme north-western corner of Aylesford parish. Millhall, at the opposite end of the parish, has the same derivation.[11] Hale Place, along the Pilgrims' Way, in a corner by Burham parish, has retained the old spelling, as has Hale, near Luton.

Victoria Road was intended to be a spinal road from Bridgewood to Luton, but this concept was never realised, and as a result of later developments only isolated sections of the road remain. The extreme western end was cut off by the M2 and even Victoria Close, just north

Plate 12   Kit Hill Avenue, on a wet late autumn day in 1994.
(Photograph by Heather Kavanagh.)

of the M2 roundabout, vanished. Of the next section, from the M2 to Taddington Valley, part was destroyed when the peripheral road (Walderslade Woods Road) was constructed in 1976, and part was 'captured' by Hallsfield as an access onto the peripheral road — Halls-field simultaneously losing its direct vehicular access onto the A229. The rest of this section was destroyed when Papion Close was built in 1980. East of Taddington Valley, the present Victoria Road maintains both the line of the road and its name. Beyond this, the section which plunged down Dallen's Bank into Walderslade Village was never more than a footpath. From Walderslade Road to Prince Charles' Avenue it still exists, though now known as Prince's Avenue. Mr Brake never established the final length, from Prince Charles' Avenue to Luton, but thereby hangs a story which is outside the scope of this book.

Victoria Road was less successful than Hallsfield in opening up land for development, possibly because there were a number of small-holdings fronting it. Brake Estate roads were typically wide and straight, but surfacing and maintenance were the responsibility of the frontagers. If they did not bother — and anyone with a long frontage might not — or if, as in some instances, they emigrated in search of work, the road was not maintained. Consequently, Brake Estate Roads varied from fair (rough, but passable, even in wet weather, Kit Hill Avenue being an example (*Plate 12*)), to Sloughs of Despond, which, in wet weather, were impassable to pedestrians and vehicles alike. Victoria Road and the northern half of Tunbury Avenue were notorious. Indeed, the overall effect of the Brake Estates' activities was less than might have been expected. Generally speaking, land fronting the roads slowly developed, but back land did not. In 1972, KCC obtained a Compulsory Purchase Order on 415 acres (168ha) of land for residential development. Most of this lay within the 508 acres (205ha) which Mr Brake had purchased 70 years before.

The first buses ran through Blue Bell Hill in 1908, being operated by a private company owned by French of Maidstone. In 1914, it was taken over by Maidstone and District Motor Services Ltd, who made Maidstone–Chatham (later Maidstone–Gillingham) their number one route. In the *Chatham, Rochester and Gillingham News* of 1st May 1915, we find them advertising:

> ### Additional Journeys now running Daily.
> *Leave Maidstone ... 7am*
> *Leave Chatham ... 8am*

Buses were popular with people in rural areas: in an area such as Blue Bell Hill, they could save a dockyard worker a three mile (4.8km) walk to the tram terminus by Chatham Cemetery. (The bus lay-by adjacent the Football Ground is the old turning circle for the trams.) They were less popular with Highway Boards. In June 1914, the Roads Management Committee of Malling Rural District Council resolved to approach Maidstone Motor Bus Company, "with a view to terms being arrived at to meet the extra expense caused by such services ...".[12] There is no subsequent reference to this in the minutes. This may be because war halted the expansion of the bus company, or it may be because there are long gaps in the committee minutes between November 1916 and April 1919. Once the war was over, the problem re-asserted itself. In 1922, the Committee instructed their Surveyor to obtain estimates for making up the bus route from Aylesford to Wouldham. The Surveyor duly presented them with estimates for the phenomenal sum of £9,000. Blue Bell Hill was in a privileged position. The Maidstone–Chatham Road had been taken over by the County Council in 1867, and hence was maintained out of the larger resources of the County Council.[13]

It is worth remembering that during the period 1900–1920, the accepted method of making up roads was basically the age-old technique of placing stones in the road, up-dated by then rolling them and spraying them with pitch. This was not without its problems. In hot weather, the pitch melted, and everybody and everything stuck to it, while in August 1923 we find the unfortunate Roads Committee of Malling RDC coping with an indignant complaint that the "tar was polluting the fresh-water streams". Traction engines also caused trouble, as the roads had insufficient foundations to take their weight.

The final decade of the period we are considering was marred by tragedy. There was the national — indeed, international — tragedy of a war which ought never to have occurred. There was local tragedy arising from it; in particular, whenever a Chatham-based ship went down, a high proportion of grieving relatives could be found in the district. There was a tragedy specific to Blue Bell Hill, in the death of Emily Trigg.[14] Emily, 20 years old, petite, pretty, was in service in Rochester with Miss Cooper. On Sunday 16th August 1916, she left the house to visit her mother for Sunday tea. She never arrived. Six weeks later, her body was found near a track which led from the Rochester–Maidstone Road to Buckmore Park, where it had been left by whoever assaulted and murdered her.

The Triggs were a respectable working class family. They lived in Prospect Row, a small terrace of cottages between the Chapel and Bridgewood Cottage. Kate Trigg was the widow of a quarryman, and mother of a large family. Sons, William, Fred and John, were in the Army in France; since they were not Privates, but Sergeant, Corporal and Lance-Corporal, we can surmise that they were 'Regulars'. The Army, Navy and Dockyard were three of the main employers in the area; many young men, faced with the choice between unemployment on one hand, and military or naval service on the other, chose the latter. A fourth son lived next-door to his mother. There were at least two girls, in addition to Emily; the youngest still lived at home.

Emily was dutiful. She had two evenings off every week, and visited her mother twice weekly. When she did not arrive home on the fateful Sunday, Mrs Trigg assumed that she had been kept at work for the following day, when her mistress had arranged to entertain some convalescent soldiers. Such loss of free time was an accepted part of being 'in service', the occupation to which most young girls were committed when they left school at 14 years. Conversely, although Miss Cooper waited up for a time before going to bed, she assumed that Emily was staying at home for the night, as she had done on a previous occasion. We can imagine that she was irritated by the lack of domestic help on the Monday, when her niece had to help with the chores involved in entertaining the soldiers. Not until Tuesday morning was the alarm raised, when Mrs Trigg walked to Rochester with Emily's clean clothes, as was her wont, and mother and mistress discovered that Emily had vanished.

Mrs Trigg reported to the police that Emily was missing, but no further action was taken. Family and friends knew her as quiet and respectable. To the police, not knowing her, there were several reasons why a young servant girl should go missing. She may have run away. She may have been 'in trouble', and not wanted her family to know. She may have decided that she could make more money by going 'on the streets' — there was, after all, plenty of scope in a naval and military town. To her mother and family, none of these merited consideration. We can only imagine the anguish of those six weeks of uncertainty, before it was replaced with the greater agony of knowing that she had been brutally murdered.

The story is given greater poignancy by the knowledge that, when she set out on that fateful Sunday, she was wearing the new best clothes made four months previously for her brother's wedding. Blue suit — her youngest sister had an identical suit; almost certainly these were home-made — white muslin blouse, black stockings, new boots, white hat, trimmed with roses and black velvet ribbons, and — the essence of Edwardian respect-ability — cotton gloves, one of which was still on her hand when her body was found. No-one was ever charged with her murder, neither was the exact cause of death established. The trail was six weeks old by the time her body was found. It was war-time, with a vast number of soldiers and sailors passing through Chatham and Rochester — if, indeed, her assailant was not a local person. The blood-and-mud bath of the 1916 Somme offensive was at its height. Zeppelins were bombing London and Kent. And Emily was, after all, only a working class girl! Let us, almost a century on, remember her with compassion, as a young Blue Bell Hill girl who, had she lived, might even now have been a respected nonagenarian in the Village.

Chapter Three – References
The Village Develops
1820–1920

1) CTR 52 B Kent Archives Office, Burham Tithe Map
   CTR 52 A Kent Archives Office, Burham Tithe Assessment
2) West, Jenny, **The Windmills of Old Kent**, published Chas Shilton T Ltd, 1973.
3) Register of Electors, 1868–1869, Mid-Kent Division, Maidstone Polling District.
4) U 1516/T2 Kent Archives Office, Will of Ed Fowle the Elder, 1787.
5) U 886/T1 Bundle 14, Preston Hall Estate Papers — Transfer of Warren Farm, 1845.
6) Cave-Brown, J, **Notes about Boxley**, published Wickham, Week Street, 1870.
7) U861/P10 Kent Archives Office, Bensted's Map, 1863.
8) *Chatham, Rochester and Gillingham Observer*, 15th October 1892, "Zion Baptist Mission at Blue Bell Hill".
9) Oral information: Miss Q Horlock.
10) *Chatham, Rochester and Gillingham News*, 9th March 1901
    Chatham, Rochester and Gillingham Observer, 15th February 1929
    Chatham, Rochester and Gillingham Observer, 6th July 1940.
11) Glover, Judith, **The Place-names of Kent**, (entry under Millhall), published by Meresborough Books, Rainham, 1982.
12) RD/ML/Am/3/9 Kent Archives Office, Malling RDC — Roads Management Committee
13) HB/M/1 Kent Archives Office, Highways Board — Malling. Minutes of 11th November.
14) *Rochester, Chatham and Gillingham News*, 23rd September 1916.
15) Coles-Finch, W, **The Windmills of Kent**, published 1933, by A J Cassell Ltd, new impression, 1976.

Chapter Four
The Village Develops
1920–1940

Geographers tell us that, to qualify as a village, a settlement must have at least three facilities from a list which includes pub, shops, place of worship, village hall, school and playing field. Prior to 1920, Blue Bell Hill may just have qualified. Between 1920 and 1940, it came of age, with pubs, church, chapel, village hall, three shops, a forge and a petrol station, though contemporary residents did not call it a village. Those living near the main road referred to themselves as living 'on the Hill', while those living further down Robin Hood Lane referred to the area simply as 'the top of the lane'. The term 'village' slowly came into use after the M2 was built in 1962, which formed a visible boundary to the area. Newcomers are often puzzled by the designation, commenting that "It's not a real village". Prior to 1940, the facilities served a wider and more diffuse area. Some of the most active 'villagers' lived in what is now Lower Robin Hood Lane. They included Mr Walter Mills, who was active in getting St Alban's Church built; Mr Olliffe, who was Treasurer of the Village Hall Fund-raising Committee, and lived in 'Courtlands', a large house at the top of Robin Hood Hill where Olliffe's Close now lies; and Mr Jacobs, who was active in the early fêtes, and lived at 'Cartref' (now No 185) Tunbury Avenue. Whether the sense of being a village will survive the influx of new residents associated with the developments of the late 1980s remains to be seen.

The Pubs

So, what of the qualifying facilities? Pubs the village had in abundance. It owes its name to the 'Old Blew Bell', which had stood at the top of Warren Road since at least 1670, when the Burial Register of Aylesford Church records the death of a baby whose parents had come from the East End of London (Whitechapel) for hop-picking and harvesting, and were lodged at the 'Blue Bell'[1]. Although supplanted by the 'Upper Bell', the old building survived into the 20th century. Mrs Goodayle said that her father-in-law, who was born and brought up in one of the cottages above the lime-works, described it as a pair of thatched cottages.[2] 'The Robin Hood and Little John', along Common Road, was also an ancient pub. It is marked on the map published by Andrews, Drury and Herbert in 1769, and is probably much older. It stood on the drove roads from Aylesford and Burham to Rochester, and is said by Bergess and Sage to have been used by smugglers.[3] The building itself is one of the two oldest on the Hill, the other being Robin Hood House (see Chapter Six). In addition to these, the residents had the choice of the 'Bridgewood Cottage' and, if they chose to walk down the hill, the 'Lower Bell'.

Opposite the 'Upper Bell' stood a forge, a small building huddled under the bank. It had been in existence since the turn of the century. The blacksmith was Mr Hooker, who lived along Common Road.[4] The forge served a considerable catchment area, the next nearest ones being at Bredhurst and next-door to Chatham Railway Station, but by 1940 it had closed. At the opposite end of the village, as though to emphasise the difference between the traditional mode of transport and the up-and-coming motor vehicle which was replacing it, stood a petrol station. It was at the junction of Hallsfield Road with the A229, and was run by Messrs Pilcher and Holford.[5]

The Shops

There were three shops, all of which survived until recently. At the corner of Robin Hood Lane, where the block of flats called Sherwood House now stands, was Arnold's the Butcher. This was burned down one evening in March 1929.[6] An alert policeman saw smoke coming from the building, and contacted Chatham Fire Brigade. They, fortuitously, were drilling, so wasted no time in 'getting away with the motor-engine'. Upon arrival they found the interior of the premises blazing fiercely. They had a problem obtaining water, the nearest hydrant being a quarter of a mile away. They obtained permission to draw from a well on the opposite side of the road, but this ran dry after ten minutes, and the firemen, who had been reinforced by the Aylesford Brigade, could do little to prevent the flames from spreading. Mr Arnold himself was spending the evening in Rochester, consequently there was no-one in the house and hence no casualties. He was a farmer as well as a butcher, and owned the field on which the Village Hall was to be built. The shop was taken over by Chatham Co-op, who ran it as a general stores until the war.

The second shop was at No 571 on the Main Road (now Manley's) has subsequently closed. It was a newsagent's (see *Plate 13*). In the early

*Plate 13   Mr R T Gray's shop and Post Office, now Manley's, approximately 1930.
Note the board for bus timetables: buses ran at 10–15 minute intervals.
(Photograph courtesy of Mrs Madge Johnson.)*

1920s it was run by Mr R T Gray; the shop housed the village Post Office,
as it does again now. A passageway led from the front door to the rooms
at the back; a room on the left of this served as the shop, while one on
the right functioned as a doctor's surgery, being hired by Drs Richmond
and Ponder on Saturday afternoons.[7] Patients waited in the passageway,
or, when that was full, outside.[2] Prescriptions were dispensed from the
surgery at Eccles, or taken to chemists in the towns. Dr. Richmond, the
senior partner, carried out many of his rounds on horse-back, which,
considering the number of unadopted roads in the area, was probably
as good a way to travel as any.[2] Dr. Ponder lived at Sandling; father and
son provided two generations of medical care to the people of Blue Bell
Hill and Walderslade. They were a musically talented family who, for
their own enjoyment, initiated an amateur orchestra in their own home,
which is still in existence, though it has now moved to Maidstone.[8]

In 1931, Mr Laurie Gray moved into a house that had just been
built a short distance from his father's newspaper shop. For several
years he ran a drapery and haberdashery business from the garage
behind it, ably and loyally assisted by Mrs Gray. He gradually built up
a round which extended into the Weald. In 1938, the frontage of the

Plate 14 *The old shop in Robin Hood Lane (1994).*

house was altered, and in 1939, when, due to wartime rationing, he could no longer obtain petrol for the round, he switched to selling groceries.[7] His son, Mr Brian Gray, would later take over the shop and run it until 1987, when it closed and was demolished to make room for development. The shop housed the Post Office for much of this period, and was noted for the high quality of the goods sold.

In addition to the three shops in the village itself, there were two outlying ones. Brick-on-Edge Cottage, at the junction of the Pilgrims' Way with the A229, was for a time a green-grocer's.[9] Along Robin Hood Lane, adjacent the path through Taddington Valley, was Mrs Brimstead's shop, called the Horse-Shoe Stores (see *Plate 14*). It was noted among local children for selling two-penny ('tuppenny' or 'tup'ny') tins of Nestlé's condensed milk. One of these, purchased with the pooled resources of several children, and poured over stewed apples, which had been 'scrumped' from the gardens of empty houses, and cooked in a disreputable old saucepan over a camp fire in the woods, was Food for the Gods. Why we didn't all die of food poisoning is beyond my understanding. This shop was effectively put out of business by the rationing system which operated during the war, and the austerity period which followed it. There was little profit to be made out of serving a small population with their weekly two ounces of butter, two ounces of marg and two ounces of cheese, and the limited amount of tinned and packeted food which could be obtained with 'points'. (Two ounces is 56 grammes.)

The Village Hall[10]

Fund-raising began in the early 1920s. In 1923, a committee was set up to organise a village fête, the committee members being Captain Kenny, Lieutenant Biddle RN, Mr Barling, Mr Drew, Mrs Gray, Mrs Barling, Mrs Kirk and Mrs Wilmshurst. The Secretary was Mr Gray, whom we have already met as the owner of the newsagent's, and who would prove to be the main organiser and driving force. The fête was held in the meadow behind the shop; proceeds were donated to Kent County Ophthalmic Hospital.[11] The following year, another fête was held which raised over £30 (a substantial sum in those days) in aid of the St John Ambulance Transport Division. It was opened by Mr Wallace A Watson, a local solicitor who lived in 'Fairview', Common Road, and was "well-known for his interest in all matters pertaining to charities".[12] He also had a considerable interest in the new technology of 'moving films'; the garden of 'Fairview' is said to have been designed as a background for amateur theatricals and films.[13]

The third fête (1925) was formally opened by the Vice-President, Mr Jacobs. Mr Gray then announced that this year "it had been decided to use the money in purchasing a piece of land for the erection of a recreation room, as the inhabitants of the district have no hall or room in which to hold meetings or social gatherings. They had also decided to call the room the Wallace Watson Memorial in memory of the late Mr Wallace Watson ...".[14] This name was retained by the Charity Commissioners when the hall was registered with them in 1954, though a minute of 1953 records a resolution that it be known as Blue Bell Hill Village Hall and this is current practice.

The land was purchased from Will Arnold in 1927,[15] the Trustees being Mrs Lillie Watson, Mrs Needham and Messrs. Hardy, Olliffe, Gray, Barling and Denne.[10] The first hall — a small wooden hut — was opened in 1928 (*Plate 15*), and the first annual general meeting was held on 11th January 1929, when the Steering Committee formally handed over the Hall to the Management Committee. The Treasurer, Mr Olliffe, reported that they owed the bank £4.7s.5d. This disgraceful state of affairs was quickly remedied — "Mrs W. A. Watson kindly handed in £1 and Mrs LeGassick as Treasurer of the Whist Drive Committee reported a balance of £4.1s.3½d in the hands of that body of workers. Cheers!"[10] The Management Committee was in business and they were solvent.

They immediately set about enlarging the Hall, resolving in 1932 to extend it by 10ft (3m) to the north and add a cloakroom to the west end. They discussed the increased maintenance charges which could arise. They drew up plans and obtained a tender of £62 for the work.

Plate 15 'A group of prime movers, whose efforts have supplied Blue Bell Hill with the much wanted village hall, photographed outside the "Wallace Watson Memorial Hall," which was opened on Monday.
'Front row (left to right): Messrs R C Gray, M J Denne, J Jones, Hardy and Barling.
'Among those behind are Mr Day, Mrs Hardy, Mrs Gray, Mrs Hills, Mrs Jones, Mrs Denne and Mrs Barling.'   (B Gray, 1928.)

Then Malling RDC unkindly withheld planning permission. It would be another 25 years before the longed-for extension was built. The early Management Committees established the tradition of prudent finance which has persisted to this day. A succession of whist drives, dances, socials, summer fêtes and jumble sales supplemented the income from hiring fees, and enabled the Hall Committee to cover its costs, keep the Hall in repair, and build up a fund to pay for the extension. The tradition of 'giving', already established by the first two fêtes, was continued. Requests for reduced booking fees for charitable events were viewed favourably. Christmas parties for local children were organised, but not allowed to become a drain on the Hall's resources, extra whist drives or jumble sales being held to finance such events. This tradition has also persisted, though now transferred to the annual fête, held on the second Saturday in June, and using the resources of the Hall and Church.

The minutes were kept meticulously, and make an interesting social record of the changes occurring in one small 20th century community. In addition to the normal problems of village halls, such as leaky roof, damaged light bulbs, hirers who fail to clear up after their event or over-run their time, broken crockery and the problem of maintaining the surround, we see new problems arising. The County Council wanted part of the land for road widening. Car parking, never mentioned before

1939, features several times in later minutes. We see the Committee receiving its first complaint about "thumping music", and a complaint about a motor-bike being driven around the field during a youth event. There were increased hirings for wedding receptions and private parties, and increased attention to insurance cover. National events were sometimes reflected, as when a committee meeting was cancelled in January 1963, "due to the arctic weather". This was the notorious winter of 1962–1963, when the Medway froze at Rochester Bridge, the sea froze at Herne Bay, the oil tanks froze at Grain Refinery and the water pipes froze in Blue Bell Hill Village Hall. Sadly, we see also a record of decreasing attendance at AGMs. In the early days, although the community was small and scattered, the residents valued their Hall and were proud of it. Latterly, with increased mobility resulting from car ownership, and increased sophistication of leisure pursuits, interest in the Hall dwindles. A small band of stalwarts soldiers on.

The only hiccup in the minutes was between 1939 and 1942. On 13th September 1939, ten days after the declaration of war, the Committee met to discuss the position of the Hall in wartime, and agreed that it should be closed temporarily, but should be available for ARP (Air Raid Precautions) if required. The library was also to carry on as usual. In February 1940 they met again to discuss re-opening the Hall and agreed to hold afternoon Whist Drives. This was a common pattern. At the beginning of the war, meeting-places were recommended to close, Government fearing the effects of air raids on buildings where many people were assembled, and where one bomb could cause many casualties. Six months later, the air raids not having materialised (yet!), lulled into a sense of false security by the 'phoney war' of the first eight months, and faced with a population which was becoming bored and demoralised by the lack of its accustomed leisure pursuits, places of entertainment began cautiously to open their doors again. Emphasis tended to be on afternoon activities because of the black-out — not that the latter would have worried the residents of Blue Bell Hill. With three lamps along the main road from the 'Upper Bell' to Bridgewood Gates, and three along the whole length of Robin Hood Lane, they were used to it. The Hall Committee functioned on an *ad hoc* basis until 1942, when it was re-formed, and the minutes, although brief, became regular again.

As indicated in the Introduction, it is not my intention to write the post-war history of the village, but it seems a bit silly to leave the Hall as a wooden hut which, to the present-day observer, it obviously is not. Therefore, to summarise briefly the development of the Hall during

Plate 16   *Blue Bell Hill Village Hall, 1990.*

the last 50 years: After the war, the Management Committee settled down once more to raise money for an extension. By 1953, the fund stood at £1,000. The Committee negotiated a grant from Kent Council for Social Services, and also a loan of £600. In 1957, the longed-for extension was built, in the shape of a new brick hall in front of the wooden one (*Plate 16*). It was opened on 21st September by Mrs Gray, the opening being celebrated by a social and a dance.

The £600 was repayable in eight years, but the Committee, ever prudent, repaid it in five-and-a-half years to reduce the interest payable. On the fifth anniversary of the opening, 21st September 1962, they celebrated the final payment of the loan with another social, then promptly embarked upon plans for a new cloakroom. This was completed by October 1963, with the help of another loan from the Council for Social Services, and with the help of Messrs Tarry and Payne, who did the plastering and plumbing, thus keeping down the cost. Finally, in 1983, under the Chairmanship of Mr Percy Harryman, the old timber hall which had served for 50-odd years was replaced by a brick-built small hall and new kitchen.

Before leaving the Hall, we should, perhaps, pay tribute to some of the people who have served it. They are a multitude, some named in the minutes, some un-named and unsung, some humble care-takers, from Mrs Keefe to the indomitable Madge Johnson, some fund-raisers and organisers. It would render this book top-heavy to quote them all by name, but of those involved prior to 1945 we should, perhaps, draw attention to:

- Mr R T Gray, who, as already described, was the driving force in the days before the Hall was built, and acted as Secretary of the Steering Committee, until he handed over to the Management Committee at the first AGM. His son, Mr Laurie Gray, would later chair the Management Committee from 1956–1965, during which time, he oversaw the building of the extension, including fund-raising by local gymkhanas, and also oversaw the registration of the Hall as a charity — a task fraught with some difficulty as most of the original trustees had died.
- Mr Walter Mills, who chaired the Steering Committee, chaired the Management Committee and set it on its path for the first two years (1921–1931), and then became instrumental in the building of St Alban's Church.
- Mr Alexander, Chairman from 1934 to 1943, and active also in the Rate-payers' Association.
- Mrs Oram, who acted as Secretary and Treasurer in the difficult days between 1942 and 1945.
- Mr Somers, Treasurer from 1930, until he was 'called up' in 1939; Secretary from 1935–1939, and who did another 'double stint' from 1948–1952. Like Mr Mills, he was also active in getting the Church built.

St Alban's Church

St Alban's was built under the Twelve Churches Scheme. This was the Diocesan response to development in North-West Kent which, even in the 1920s, was outstripping available resources. The aim was to raise £50,000 towards the cost of building churches in newly-developed areas.[16] By 1931, when St Alban's was built, the fund stood at £28,000. St Alban's was the fourth of the churches to be started, the first three being St Andrew's at Bromley, a mission hall at Bexley Heath, and a temporary church at Pett's Wood.[17]

The local driving forces were Mr Walter Mills and Mr J P Somers, as indicated at the end of the previous section. Mr Somers, in addition to his work on the Hall Committee, was Treasurer of the Church Building Committee. He was very well liked and respected; local residents who knew him still speak of him with affection. In the chancel of the Church stands a simple wooden throne-chair, dedicated to his memory. Mr Walter Mills lived in what is now Lower Robin Hood Lane, and was Secretary of the Church Building Committee. The contemporary account of the dedication service records that " ... the establishment of the Church has been largely due to Mr W T Mills who has ... been working in the district for the last few years as a lay-reader ... Owing to illness he was unable to attend the dedication".[18]

The Anglican Church had been active in the area, even before St Alban's was built. Like the Baptist Chapel forty years earlier (see Chapter Three), its first services were held in a private house, being led by Rev R L Ryan in a room lent by Mr and Mrs R T Gray.[19] After one of the fêtes in the 1920s, it was suggested that as the 'big tent' would not be taken down until Monday, a church service might be held in it on Sunday afternoon. Mr R T Gray invited Canon Everett, the Rural Dean, to conduct the service.[20] It was so well attended, and so much appreciated, that he was asked to make arrangements to hold a regular weekly service in the Village Hall when this was available. He duly appointed Mr Walter Mills to be responsible for the proper organisation and conduct of the services. Fittings which could be set up and taken down again quickly and easily, were kindly lent by a naval chaplain, and as soon as the Village Hall was opened, it was booked for Sunday Service.[20] A list of the hiring charges given in the minutes of the first Annual General Meeting of the Hall includes a charge of 2/6 for this purpose.[10] This can be compared with 5/– for private functions, and 15/– for political meetings, which the Hall Committee seems traditionally to have rated low on its list of priorities. By the time the foundation stone was laid, local people had already collected £90 towards the cost of the Church. This was a remarkable effort, considering that the community had only just finished collecting money for the Hall. The Church was expected to cost £1,570. £225 had already been paid for the land. Another £40 was received from the collections and donations made at the stone-laying ceremony, £70 was promised by the Incorporated Church Building Scheme, and £1,000 was to come from the Twelve Churches Scheme.[21] The fact that there was already a nucleus of a congregation helped to persuade the Diocesan Authorities to contribute to it.

The foundation stone was laid on 27th July 1931 by Mrs Donald Tait, wife of Archdeacon Tait of Rochester.[21] By October, the Church was completed, and the Service of Dedication was held on Saturday 30th October.[17] The Architect was Mr Goring, and his concept of the Church was forward-looking. The vestry was intended to be used for small meetings, a function which it still performs. A shutter was fixed "so that the Chancel can be shut off from the main body of the building, thus forming a hall for secular entertainment". This idea was revolutionary at the time, though common-place nowadays. A large lantern screen was provided, and the nave was intended to seat 120. Mr Goring further designed the Church "in rural style to harmonise with its surroundings". Sixty years on, most local residents would agree that he was successful in achieving this aim (*Plate 17*). The builder was Mr Leech, a local lay-reader who was popular at the Mission Church of St James in Walderslade.

The new Church was given a number of gifts, including a pulpit, chalice and ewer from Underriver, a small font, an organ and benches from St Michael's at Stone, a cross and pair of candle-sticks from St Luke's in Bromley (itself to be destroyed in an air raid ten years later) and a lectern, the latter commemorating Bishop and Mrs Harmer's interest in the Girls' Friendly Society, though it is not clear why St Alban's was chosen for this particular honour. At the dedication service, the robed clergy included Rev Johnson "in whose parish the mission area partly lies". Rev Johnson was Rector of Chatham, from which we can deduce that the new Church was intended to serve the Davis Estate, which lay in Chatham. Walderslade Village, which also lay in Chatham parish, already had its own mission church. The singing was led by Aylesford Church Choir, with Mr W E Wilson at the organ. The service included Psalm 122 and the Old Hundredth. The following day, there was a service of Holy Communion in the morning, and a thanksgiving service in the afternoon, followed by the first christening in the new Church — Lilian Ethel Smith, aged three months.

In 1993, 70 years on, St Alban's continues to flourish. The main body of the Church is used for social activities, as envisaged by the architect. Residents of Davis Estate still use the Church, though they now have the choice of St Stephen's at Hunstman's Corner. The Church is still served by a band of devoted workers. The annual fête, on the second Saturday in June, brings together the resources of Church and Village Hall in the tradition of self help and charitable giving; in the ten years between 1979 and 1989, the fêtes raised a total of £4,000 for distribution to local and other charities. Truly, Blue Bell Hill village has come of age.

The Rate-payers' Association[22]

Traditionally an English village is the centre of a parish, administratively, if not geographically. Blue Bell Hill village, as it developed, found itself lumbered with two parish councils, neither of which really wanted to know that it existed. Common Road, Mill Lane, Robin Hood Lane as far as the Church, and most of the main road were in Burham parish.

Plate 17 St Alban's Church, 1990.

Warren Road, most of Robin Hood Lane, the main road from where the M2 now lies, to the boundary with Chatham, and all Brake Estate roads, including Hallsfield, were in Aylesford parish. It is, therefore, not surprising that a Rate-payers' Association developed to act as a pressure group, and to co-ordinate representations to the two parish councils and to the Rural District Council. The minutes of the Association date from 1929, when they held their AGM in the new Village Hall, but the Association probably existed before this. There was considerable overlap between the personnel of the Rate-payers' Association and the Management Committee of the Hall — though the Rate-payers' Association had no ladies on its committee! After all, women had been entitled to the vote for only ten years: it was obviously unreasonable to expect them to understand the intricacies of Local Government! The duplication of personnel gave rise to some confusion, so that we find matters of general interest being raised at AGMs of the Hall, or even at ordinary Management Committee meetings.

Some things have changed so little that one feels like quoting "there's nothing new under the sun". Thus, in September 1929, it is minuted that "Mr Alexander called attention to the lack of scavenging on the Hill although rates are paid for the same as [in] the village". His view was supported. In February 1932, they arranged to lobby the respective parish councils. Messrs Biddle, Clerke, Kite and Parks were to attend Aylesford Parish Council, and Messrs Hardy, Somers, Mayger and Alexander (Chairman) were to attend Burham Parish Council. Other rate-payers were urged to join them. No report of the meeting is minuted, but in May 1932 it was agreed that the Secretary should write and ask when scavenging (litter-picking) was likely to commence.

In the 1980s, scavenging — or lack of it — was still a source of aggravation, only now it was parish councils who tried to persuade District and Borough Councils to scavenge parished areas as well as urban ones.

Another topic that is still with us is the condition of roads and footways. Robin Hood Lane featured prominently. In 1932 the Rate-payers agreed that " ... the attention of Malling RDC be called to the unsatisfactory condition and heavy and increasing use of the road and requesting that immediate steps be taken to utilise the land given to the Council by Mr Brake by construction of a road of full dimensions the moment being opportune [as] many of the unemployed could find work there-on; failing this the provision of a footpath as pedestrians, children especially, were in daily danger from fast traffic on the narrow road". Sixty years on, we can, perhaps, smile indulgently at the references to 'heavy use' and 'fast traffic'. The narrowness, however, was not an exaggeration. For most of the distance between the Church and where the footbridge over Walderslade Woods Road now stands, the trees met overhead. Two cars — or a car and pony-and-trap — could not pass, except at passing places. Pressure for the road to be widened dated back to at least 1923, when a deputation of two, chosen to represent both the Burham and Aylesford parts of the community, met Malling Highways Management Committee to ask for the road to be widened. They pointed out that the passing places were unsatisfactory "owing to the spongy nature of the subsoil".[23] They were unsuccessful, the request coinciding with the estimates for making up roads used as bus routes, referred to in Chapter Three, though the Highways Committee did agree to consider improving the passing places. By the late 1930s, local residents had partly solved the footpath problem by treading out an unsurfaced path through the edge of the woods on the north side of the road, separated from the road by a narrow belt of trees and shrubs (*Plate 18*). The land along this side slopes away from the road, so that the path was at a slightly lower level than the road. The modern footway still reflects this origin. The trees and shrubs (and their accompanying spring flowers) have disappeared, and the narrow belt of trees is now a grass verge, but between Nos 244–260 and Nos 270–308, the footway is still below the level of the road, where an

Plate 18   *Robin Hood Lane, approximately 1930, about where the footbridge over
Walderslade Woods Road now stands. Note the rough footpath near
the left-hand edge, which ran from this point near St Alban's Church.
Further up the lane there were many more bushes and small trees in
the verge, so that the path was completely hidden from the road.*
(Photograph courtesy of Mrs Madge Johnson.)

earlier generation of Hill-dwellers trod it out through the edge of the
woods, and although it is metalled the tarmac overlies the earth of a
woodland path, so that the surface is still uneven.

Street lighting also exercised the Rate-payers. In 1928, they agreed
to write to Aylesford Parish Council pointing out that Burham Parish
Council had done its part by lighting the Upper Bell Corner, and the
junction of Robin Hood Lane with the main road, and requesting that
three lights be provided along Aylesford's portion of the lane. This
stretched from St Alban's Church to just east of Tunbury Avenue. In
December, they had a site meeting with representatives of the parish
council, who seemed sympathetic. In April, they wrote to remind the
parish council that a decision was awaited. In June, they received a
distinctly caustic reply, advising them to "try to obtain parish council
power of their own under Chatham instead of Malling when they could
spend their own lighting rates on road lighting to their own requirements." In the event, some lights were eventually installed; these were,
of course, gas lamps. As children in the mid-1930s, we would some-

times wait on short winter afternoons for the lamp-lighter to arrive on his bicycle at the corner of Tunbury Avenue, carrying the long pole which, pushed into the lamp, mysteriously lit it. Documents in the possession of Aylesford Parish Council make it clear that he returned at 11pm to turn it off again — it was a thrifty age. The lamp-lighter was that same Mr Jack Trigg from Common Road, whom we have already met as care-taker of Blue Bell Hill Chapel.

Other matters which exercised the Rate-payers included water supply and water rates, which will be described in the next chapter, noxious weeds and schooling. Concern over noxious weeds indicates how rural the area still was. In 1928, they complained to Mr Brake's agent about "the condition of unoccupied land in the parish; weeds of all descriptions, thistles especially, grow profusely and seeds blow about in all directions, to the distress of all good gardeners and contrary to the Act". Much of the unoccupied land was unsold land of the Brake Estates. Mr Brake, through his agent Mr Sharman, denied responsibility (8/4/29), so the Rate-payers reported the matter to the Crop Reporter, who, in reply, promised to give the matter of seeding weeds his attention at the proper time. The Crop Reporter, unexpectedly, functioned under the aegis of the Board of Education. There are no further minutes on the matter, though warnings may have been circulated, as the writer can remember her father's anxiety that thistles and docks should not go to seed, either in the garden or on the verge of the road for which, it being a Brake Estate road, he was responsible.

With regard to schooling, throughout the period, the Rate-payers tried to persuade the education authority to provide a school on the Hill. The answer was always the same — there were insufficient children to justify a separate school. KEC did acquire land for the purpose, presumably envisaging future development, but in 1985 the village by-pass cut through this land. Some of the children attended Burham Primary Schools; older residents remember the lorry which took them to Burham. Others went to Darget's Road School in Walderslade. By the 1930s, there was a private school in the village, run by Miss Brewer.[7,9] It was in the house adjacent the old entrance to Buckmore Park; she catered for children between the ages of five and eleven. After the age of eleven years, they went to various schools. Those who passed the 'scholarship exam' (now known as the 11+) went to Chatham Girls' Grammar, Gillingham Boys' Grammar or to the Rochester schools — Kings, Sir Joseph Williamson's Mathematical School or Rochester Girls' Grammar. Most of the others went to Ordnance Street or Highfields, from which, at thirteen plus, some transferred to Technical Schools. Already, by 1929, there was a school bus; the Rate-payers complained that the children were not being set down at the correct place. The contractor for this bus was Buck's Coaches. Later, the children were issued with season tickets for use on service buses; this led to the Rate-payers complaining in 1946 that children from Highfields and Ordnance Street schools could not get on the buses in the afternoons. This was, in fact, a common problem at the time as the buses filled up in Chatham and few people alighted before they reached Huntsman's Corner.

The period after 1945 is outside the remit of this book. Suffice it to say that, between 1945 and 1950, the Rate-payers made valiant efforts to ensure that residents on the Hill were represented on their respective parish councils. Both parishes were eventually granted separate wards for the area on the Hill, thus ensuring representation and bringing to an end the need for an association which had served the community energetically and conscientiously during the development of the village. At the 1972 Local Government re-organisation — that disastrous epidemic of shot-gun marriages contracted between unwilling councils and witnessed by an uncomprehending public — it was assumed that the area would be transferred into Chatham — or Medway Towns, to use the characterless and mechanical nomenclature which has resulted in Chatham's history and individuality being submerged in that of Rochester. The County Council and District Councils drew up their recommendations on that basis. They reckoned without Blue Bell Hill. The residents attended the appropriate meeting of Malling RDC en masse; a grim-faced phalanx in the public seats making clear their emotionally-determined wish (the logic of their view was less clear) to remain with their ancient parishes in the new district of Tonbridge & Malling.[24] The politicians on the District Council 'chickened out' and voted against transferring them to Chatham. Finally, in 1988 the Burham portion of the village was transferred to Aylesford parish, thus altering the age-old boundary laid down in Jutish times.

Chapter Four — References
The Village Develops
1920–1940

1)   PL12/1/1 Kent Archives Office. Burial Registers of Aylesford Parish Church.

2)   Oral information: Mrs Goodayle, Collingwood Road.

3)   Bergess W and Sage S, **Five Medway Villages**, published by Meresborough Books, Rainham, 1983.

4)   Oral information: Mr A Keefe, Maidstone Road, Bridgewood.

5)   Oral information: Mr P Harryman, Maidstone Road, Bridgewood.

6)   *Chatham, Rochester & Gillingham Observer*, 22nd March 1929.

7)   Oral information: Mr B Gray, Hallsfield Road, Bridgewood.

8)   History of the Old Barn Orchestral Society, 1927-1970.

9)   Oral information: Mr P Sandford, Warren Road.

10)   Minutes of the Blue Bell Hill Village Hall. Unpublished.

11)   Newspaper cutting in the possession of Mr B Gray.

12)   *Rochester, Chatham & Gillingham Observer*, 18th July 1924.

13)   Oral information: Mrs Sue Taylor, Common Road.

14)   *Rochester, Chatham & Gillingham Observer*, 31st July 1925.

15)   Official Charity Commission Scheme, 1954.

16)   *Rochester, Chatham & Gillingham Observer*, 24th July 1931; 31st July 1931.

17)   *Rochester, Chatham & Gillingham Observer*, 23rd October 1931.

18)   *Rochester, Chatham & Gillingham Observer*, 30th October 1931.

19)   Notes written by Mr R T Gray, in the possession of Mr B Gray. Unpublished.

20)   Pamphlet written by Mr W T Mills and endorsed by Canon Everett, February 1938 (kindly loaned by Mr B Gray).

21)   *Rochester, Chatham & Gillingham Observer*, 31st July 1931.

22)   Minutes of Blue Bell Hill Rate-payers' Association. Unpublished.

23)   RD/ML/Am/3/9 Kent Archives Office. Malling RDC — Roads Management Committee. Minutes of April 4th 1923.

24)   Oral information: Cllr Mr A Craven, Warren Road.

Chapter Five
The Tale of a Tank

Local people know the old water tank along Common Road. For seventy years, it has stood there, square, silent, severely functional, its long metal legs planted firmly in its neat little plot of land. Everyone takes it for granted, but how came it into existence?

The great cholera epidemics of 1848 and the early 1850s in which, nationally, 100,000 people died, had drawn attention to the connection between these outbreaks and inadequate water supplies, though it would be another 40 years before the work of Cohn, Koch and Pasteur laid the foundation of the germ theory of infectious disease. The outbreaks resulted in a series of public health measures, and a large number of private Acts authorising commercial companies to supply water to large towns. Maidstone Water-Works Company was set up in 1860 to supply water to the town,[1] the population of which had increased from 8,000 in 1801, to 23,000 in 1861. Nearly thirty years later, in 1888, Mid-Kent Water Company was established, being authorised to construct a well, pumping station, reservoir and ancillary works at Halling, and to supply water to the adjacent parishes of Snodland, Ryarsh, Birling, Addington, Leybourne, Ditton and West Malling.[2]

In 1883, there had been a serious epidemic of typhoid in Eccles, followed by less serious ones in each of the next three years. Malling Union Rural Sanitary Authority (one of the forerunners of the district council), therefore asked the company to extend its area of supply to the parishes of Wouldham, Burham and Aylesford, which included Eccles. In 1890, even before they had completed the works at Halling, the company duly sought permission to extend their sphere of operations and began the necessary consultations. The Sanitary Authority were obviously in favour of it, the Highways Board agreed, and so did the Vestry Meetings (forerunners of the parish councils) of Burham and Wouldham. Aylesford Vestry Meeting dug in their heels and objected.

The trouble had its origin in the rebuilding of Preston Hall, some forty years earlier. The ancient seat of Preston Hall had for centuries been occupied by the Culpepper family, but the local branch had died out in the 18th century.[3] In 1848, the Hall and estates were purchased by Edward Ladds-Bett, a noted civil engineer. He knocked down the old house, erected a new one, and proposed to install a water supply by piping water from the springs at Great Tottington. This upset the residents of Aylesford, who complained that by abstracting water at source he was interfering with their public rights on the stream, which runs from Great Tottington to Aylesford village, there to empty into the Medway. In 1858, they took him to court and won their case.[4] However, by a judicious blend of dire warning — "When the cholera now raging on the continent reaches this country you will regret having only an open stream as a water supply" — and plain bribery — "If you withdraw your objections I will erect 6 stand-pipes in the village from which you may draw clean water, free" — he eventually overcame their opposition. Preston Hall obtained its water supply, and so did Aylesford village. For the next thirty years, they enjoyed a water supply which, by the standards of its time, was remarkably pure, and cost them nothing.

Mid-Kent Water Company's proposals were seen as a threat to this comfortable arrangement. Preston Hall had by now passed to the Brassey family. Mr Brassey feared that the Company's activities would cause his springs to dry up. The Vestry Meeting, one suspects, merely wanted to maintain the status quo. Despite repeated assurances from the company, no agreement could be reached, so on 23rd March 1890, they all trooped into the Brassey Rooms in Aylesford village and held a public enquiry.[5]

The Solicitor for the Company urged that the consent of the Aylesford Vestry meeting be dispensed with, in view of "the unsatisfactory nature of the supply at Eccles, where water is obtained from shallow wells in close proximity to the houses and cess-pits and where in 1883 there was a bad outbreak of typhoid fever. The Company did not wish to interfere with Mr Brassey's springs and would agree any reasonable clause for their protection". The Medical Officer of Health for West Kent, the Clerk to the Rural Sanitary Authority, and the District Medical Officer all supported the Company's application. A solitary farmer with a mind of his own, one Mr Hoppy by name, wanted a better water supply. The Resident Engineer to the Company, Mr A F Bowker, emphasised that the invitation to extend the limits came from the Rural Sanitary Authority, and gave an assurance that the Company proposed to obtain water from a well 375ft deep (114m), which tapped the water in the greensand, and that these deep wells could not interfere with Mr Brassey's springs, which issued from below the chalk. The local Engineer to the Company, Mr Wm Russ, was more outspoken. He had attended at least one Vestry Meeting in an attempt to reach a solution. He now declared roundly that he considered the Company's water "to be much better and he wouldn't have Mr Brassey's water if he could get it". One has the impression that he had had enough, and more than enough of Mr Brassey and the Aylesford Vestry Meeting, and could cheerfully have consigned them to the bottom of the 375ft (114m) well.

The opposition was led by the Vicar. He considered that the necessity for a further supply to Eccles had not been proved, that the Medical Officer of Health was referring to a state of affairs in past years which had been remedied, and that the death rate in Eccles was less than in other parts of the parish or in Burham. As he held the livings of both Aylesford and Burham, he was the acknowledged expert on mortality rates. He based his case on figures for one year, 1888, when there had been ten deaths in Eccles out of a population of 1,700. As witnesses, he called Mr Butler, Manager of Burham Cement Works and owner of twelve houses in Eccles, Mr Hawkes Junior, owner of one house in Eccles, Mr Hawkes Senior (thirty houses) and Mr Hammond (ten houses). All stated that "they strongly objected to the entry of the Company and were quite prepared to take steps to obtain a supply of water if the Sanitary Inspector proved it was necessary" — a condition which, in the days before the science of bacteriology developed, was almost impossible to fulfil. No other resident of Eccles is reported. Presumably they were all busy in Culand Pit, or the cement works, or cooking dinner with water drawn from the suspect wells.

Mr Brassey's case was presented by Mr Rose, of Messrs Rose, Norton and Rose, and was based on the possible danger to the springs at Tottington and Cossington. Their client only wanted a reasonable clause to protect the springs. They considered that water could easily be taken to Eccles from Tottington Springs. As witness they called Mr W Ware, Engineer to Maidstone Water-Works Company, who supported their contention that the springs "might be tapped by any operation behind them". The Maidstone company also objected on their own behalf, being represented by their solicitor. Their objection obviously came as a shock to the Mid-Kent Company, who, in their reply to the submission, commented (a little sourly, one suspects) that they did not know until the day of the enquiry that Maidstone Water-Works Company would appear to object, and hoped that a clause satisfactory to them and to Mr Brassey could be arranged.

The Inspector, Major F A Marindin, RE, CEG, in his conclusions considered that although the Company had agreed to exclude all Mr Brassey's estates, they had not shown sufficient cause for the inclusion of the rest of the parish, which effectively meant Eccles, in their area of supply. At the same time, he reported, "I don't think that a supply such as that at Eccles can be other than unsatisfactory and I trust that steps may be taken to investigate the state of the wells, which it appears have not been examined for some years. If they be still contaminated, which is denied, there would be no difficulty in arranging for a proper supply to be laid on from Tottington Springs, by the use of a ram, and the inhabitants of Eccles expressed their willingness to take steps for such a supply if it was found necessary".

The Board of Trade (Railway Department!) endorsed the Inspector's recommendation, but the argument rumbled on. In 1895, there was a second public enquiry,[4] following abortive discussion between the Rural Sanitary Authority and Mid-Kent Water Company. Malling Rural District Council had just come into existence under the 1894 Local Government Act. The Sanitary Inspector pointed out that, despite the assurance given at the earlier enquiry, the residents of Eccles had done nothing to provide themselves with a water supply, that Tottington Springs were no longer available as a source, that the Company had done nothing to supply Burham or Wouldham under the permission granted five years before, and that the need for a clean water supply in Eccles was now urgent. The Inspector accordingly recommended that the Company be given permission to extend its area of supply to Aylesford parish, without the consent of the parish council, but that permission be conditional upon the supply to Eccles being installed within two years. With the Maidstone company poised to take over if they failed to act this was no empty threat. By 1897, Eccles had its water supply.

Meanwhile, Blue Bell Hill was still high and dry. New houses were being built steadily. The Ordnance Survey map of 1898 marks a well against each of a number of houses in Common Road. These were brick-lined wells, which collected water from the roof, together with soot, cement dust and a goodly proportion of any debris which had landed on the roof since the last rain shower. All this washed into the well, which had to be cleaned regularly if the water was to be kept sweet. In wet summers, the wells remained full, so could not be cleaned. In dry summers, they could be emptied and cleaned but the houses lost their water supply. Understandably, the residents of Blue Bell Hill became restive. In March 1912, they asked for the matter of a water supply to be debated at the Annual Parish Meeting.[4] The request was signed by the requisite ten rate-payers to ensure it was on the agenda, including Mr Sandford, who owned the cottages along Warren Road, Mr Brake who considered that a proper water supply would encourage the development of his land, Mr Saunders of Robin Hood House, and Messrs Thornton, Russell-Watson and Hunnisett, all from Tunbury Avenue.

They seem to have carried the Annual Parish Meeting with them, since in June of the same year, Malling Rural District Council sent a copy of a draft agreement between themselves and Mid-Kent Water Company to Aylesford Parish Council for comment.[4] The Company wanted a return of £200 per annum on their investment. Malling RDC calculated that, at the existing level of housing, they would receive £60. Malling RDC agreed to underwrite the loss. This was not as generous as it sounds, as the loss was to be passed on to the parishes in their general rates, in the ratio of Aylesford paying £88 and Burham £52. This was to prove a sore point with Blue Bell Hill Rate-payers' Association in years to come. The RDC also imposed a condition that, if the Company's receipts rose above £200, they were to reimburse the RDC for their subsidy. It is doubtful if this situation was ever reached.

In 1913, the Company obtained the necessary authorisation to construct a reservoir and associated works in Burham, and to erect a tank on top of the downs.[2] The 1914–1918 war then intervened, and not until 1923 was the agreement with Malling RDC completed and signed, and the works carried out. Our old square water-tank, with a capacity of 45,000 gallons (204,000 litres), and a top water-level of 635ft (193m) above sea level, was erected in 1924.[2] Burham reservoir was brought into use in 1925, together with its booster station, capable of pumping 12,000 gallons an hour (54,550 litres per hour) up to the tank. Most of the water comes from Halling, being pumped across the river through two 8in (20cm) pipes, an arrangement which was adopted in 1897 to allay Mr Brassey's fears about the effect which a deep well on this side of the river might have upon Tottington

Springs. In 1972, Mid-Kent and Maidstone companies amalgamated. Mr Huggett, ex-Maidstone Water Company, told me that since then water from Cossington may also be pumped to the tank. This water is obtained from two levels, some of it from springs and some of it from a deep well at Cossington.

We might have expected that Blue Bell Hill residents would be satisfied once the water supply was installed, but not a bit of it. The fire at the butcher's shop in 1929 highlighted the lack of fire hydrants, so the Rate-payers' Association wrote to the county council, requesting that these be installed.[6] There followed two years' abortive correspondence, of a typical 'buck-passing' pattern. The county council referred the Rate-payers to the water company, who referred them to the district council, who declined to pay the guarantee required by the Company. In 1932, the Rate-payers accepted defeat. The matter surfaced again in 1938, when war seemed imminent. The RDC were approached to find out what provision was being made for the district. Situated between the barracks at Maidstone and the barracks and dockyard at Chatham, and with an airfield less than a mile away (1.6km), the Rate-payers' concern is understandable. They must have felt that the village was a 'sitting duck' for any air raids which were slightly off course. They received little reassurance from the District Council, but Burham Parish Council helpfully offered them two fire extinguishers! It was agreed to place one near the 'Upper Bell' and one near the Chapel.

The Rate-payers were also disquieted that the water supply did not extend to all roads, and they tried to remedy this at the same time as they pressed for fire hydrants. They drew attention to the cottages and farm at the back of the 'Upper Bell', and pointed out that if the supply were extended down Warren Road, it would serve a poultry farm, a dairy farm and at least three cottages; an estimated total of about twenty people. The modern mind baulks at the concept of a dairy farm with no running water; the one in question provided milk for most of the population in what is now Blue Bell Hill village. The RDC declined to pay for extending the supply, but the owners of the farm, Barlings, must have provided it themselves, as the occupiers of the cement workers' cottages further down the road used to fetch water from the farm.[7] Hallsfield Road was having trouble with "flushing mains", though the minutes of the Rate-payers' Association do not make it clear what the problem was — lack of mains, or insufficient pressure to make the cisterns fill properly. If the latter then, like other topics on the Hill, it has remained a source of contention for a long time. In 1987, the residents opposed developments as set forth in the

Local Plan, one of their objections being inadequate water pressure and a fear that additional development would aggravate the situation.

Now that a water supply was available, cesspools became more common. Main drainage would not reach the Hill until the 1960s (in part), and the 1970s. Sewerage charges and charges for emptying cesspools became a sore point with the Rate-payers. In 1937 they received a letter from the Rating and Valuation Officer explaining that "the sewerage scheme, as in nearly every rural scheme, does not enable every house to be connected but the charge is on the Parish as a whole". With a sewerage rate of 8.59d in the pound, and a standard charge by the district council of 18/– per hour for emptying cesspools, the letter was not well received. (These figures are as given in the Rate-payers' minutes; I have not checked them, and admit to some reservations about the standard charge.) An attempt was made to put forward at the Annual Parish Meetings a resolution that a small rate be charged to cover the cost of cesspool emptying. This ignored the fact that many of the older houses had not even cesspools, but relied on more primitive methods of sanitation; the proposed resolution would have entailed their owners paying both the sewerage and the cesspool emptying rates for no benefit. In fact, the standard charge, levied by the RDC, was counter-productive in terms of improved hygiene. At a time when 50/– a week was a very good wage, there was no incentive to install cesspools in those houses which did not have them while, in those which did, the occupiers made other arrangements to empty them. Semi-rotary pumps were common in the area, stand-pipes and non-return valves were easily and cheaply installed. A couple of hours steady pumping early on a summer morning, simultaneously emptied the cesspool and watered and manured the large garden upon which many families depended for their vegetables and fruit! After the 1939–1945 war, the RDC offered a service of free emptying, once every six weeks, and a charge of 2/– per 100 gallons, if more frequent emptying was required.

With development continuing on the Hill, the Company needed to safeguard the supply. I am indebted to Mr F D Wilkinson, Divisional Manager for the Western Division of Mid-Kent Water Company, for the following information, which brings the saga of Blue Bell Hill's water supply up to date:[8]

"The small circular reservoir [next to the tank] was constructed in the early 1970s to provide additional ground storage facilities on the Blue Bell Hill site. It is our normal practice to provide storage capacity equating to the average day's consumption. The circular reservoir is a pre-stressed concrete structure with a capacity of 150,000 gallons (682,000 litres) and a top water level of 624ft (190m) above Ordnance

Datum. There is also a small booster station situated on the Burham side which is capable of lifting water from the lower storage reservoir up into the Blue Bell Hill water tower and these same boosters also supply a discrete high level area near Warren Road."

Woolman's Wood Reservoir

This is the reservoir by the Bridgewood Roundabout, facing Bridgewood Manor Hotel across the A229. It occupies the eastern end of Woolman's Wood (named on the Chatham Tithe Map as Woman's Wood), which originally stretched along the northern side of the Rochester-Maidstone Road (B2097). The water companies set up during the last century were authorised to supply water to specific areas, these being based on parishes which were still the basis of local authority. Blue Bell Hill lies at the junction of five parishes, and also on one of the highest points of the downs, so it was inevitable that it would accommodate the works of more than one company. We have already seen that the parishes of Aylesford, Burham and Wouldham, lying mainly to the south of the downs, were supplied by the Mid-Kent Company. The other two parishes, Chatham and Rochester–St Margaret's, were serviced from the north. The Brompton, Chatham, Gillingham and Rochester Water-Works Company was incorporated in the same year as Maidstone Water-Works Company (1860). The first three towns had grown at a phenomenal rate with the growth of the dockyard and the concentration of military establishments. The Company obtained extensions to its powers and the areas which it served in 1868, and again in 1898.[9] In 1905, because the "demand for water within the Company's limits of supply has of late years greatly increased", they were authorised to construct additional works, including those at Capstone, Rainham Road and — more importantly for Blue Bell Hill — the well and pumping station at Snolledge Bottom, where Walderslade Road crosses the valley. The company had already purchased land for this; in February 1902, they paid Mr Maudistley Best £150 for an acre of land and also negotiated rights to construct adits [tunnels] under the surrounding hills to collect the water, including under Weeds Wood and Burnt Hoath Wood (near Bridgewood Manor Hotel). At the same time, they constructed the reservoir at Woolman's Wood. I am indebted to Mr Setterfield, Divisional Director of Southern Water Authority, for the following information:

"The first reservoir built on this site was constructed in 1902 and was of the mass concrete type. Its storage capacity was one million gallons (4.5 million litres) and it had a top water level of 462ft (140m).

"The majority of houses are supplied with water by the use of gravity. This practice was adopted by Water Engineers so that in periods of electricity failure or whilst pumping machinery is being maintained customers do not lose their water supply. Because of this practice the reservoir can only supply houses situated about 45ft (13.7m) below its top water level. Hence the area supplied from Woolman's Wood reservoir is situated in Chatham, mainly in Maidstone Road, Davis Estate, City Way, etc."

Between 1919 and 1921 the company bought an acre of Woolman's Wood from Rochester Bridge Wardens,[11] presumably in anticipation of future requirements. This was to prove justified. Mr Setterfield again:

"In 1953 because of the growth in demand a further reservoir holding three million gallons (13.6 million litres) was constructed on the same site. This time the reservoir was built using reinforced concrete, the top water level remaining the same ... Water abstracted from Snodhurst Pumping Station has always been pumped to Woolman's Wood Reservoirs. When the second reservoir was built at Woolman's Wood ... additional water mains were laid to enable water from other sources to be pumped to the site ... Both reservoirs are still in daily use."

Before closing this Chapter, an explanation and a comment: 'Snolledge', which I have used above, is the local pronunciation of Snodhurst referred to by Mr Setterfield. The names are therefore interchangeable. The banks of Woolman's Wood reservoir are today a sanctuary for wild primroses, once common over the whole of Blue Bell Hill. Long may they flourish!

Chapter Five — References
The Tale of a Tank

1) **1860–1960 A Century of Service**. Centenary publication of Maidstone Water-works Company, published 1960.
2) Edwardd, H D, **Mid-Kent Water Company – the First 50 Years**.
3) Wells, K A E, **Preston Hall and its Owners**. Manuscript, Kent Local Studies Centre.
4) P12/32/3 Kent Archives Office. Papers relating to dispute between Mid-Kent Water Co and Aylesford Parish.
5) P12/8/4 Kent Archives Office. Papers relating to dispute between Mid-Kent Water Co and Aylesford Parish.
6) Minutes of the Blue Bell Hill Rate-payers' Association, 1929–1947. Unpublished.
7) Oral information: Mr P Sandford.
8) Letter from Mr F D Wilkinson, Divisional Manager for Western Division of Mid-Kent Water Company, 13th October 1988. Unpublished.
9) U480/E81 Kent Archives Office. Papers of the Best family. Sale of Land 15th December 1902.
10) Letter from Mr G Setterfield, Divisional Director, Southern Water Authority, 25th November 1988. Unpublished.
11) Terrier of the Rochester Bridge Wardens.

Chapter Six
Where Was Eccles?

Eccles was one of the ancient manors of Aylesford, along with Tottington and the royal manor of Aylesford itself. All three pre-date the Norman conquest. Residents of both modern Eccles and Blue Bell Hill may, however, be surprised by Hasted's statement that "the site of the manor of Eccles is at present unknown but is supposed to be somewhere at the eastern extremity of [Aylesford] parish near Boxley Hill".[1] We have already seen in Chapter One, that Boxley Hill was the 18th century name for Warren Road, and indeed Hasted marks it on his map about where Blue Bell Hill Farm now stands. It therefore seems that Eccles was somewhere on Blue Bell Hill. So where exactly was it?

Hasted gives us further information. He indicates that by the late 18th century the manor had become divided between several owners. Part of it had passed to the Earl of Aylesford. As he also possessed The Friars and the whole manor of Burham, this was probably the portion from which modern Eccles derived its name. Another portion had "become vested" in the same owners as the manor of Tottington. This was not surprising. Both manors were granted by William the Conqueror to his half-brother, Odo, but the two later fell out, and Odo's territories were confiscated. Tottington and Eccles were re-allocated to Malgerius de Rokefle (Ruxley) and had similar histories. Hasted then continues: "Another part of it was lately held by Mr John Corrall and another considerable part of it ... was purchased by Mr Thos Best of Chatham ...".

Hasted was writing between 1781 and 1801. If we jump fifty years to the Tithe Apportionment of 1841, we find the executors of Mr P Corrall in possession of two parcels of land on the Hill.[2] These were North Wood and part of Impton. North Wood, five acres, fronted onto Robin Hood Lane between St Alban's Church and the M2. It had the same depth as the land on which the church now stands. Behind it lay Gredhurst Wood, with Taddington and Hurst Hill Woods adjoining, owned by Mr Thos F Best. Impton was the large wood south of Robin

Plate 19 *Pond in Impton Wood, approximately 1978, just before development commenced. Note the marker oak at the extreme right-hand side. The steepest part of the bank, and the deepest part of the pond, was at this end; at the opposite end the banks flattened out and the pond became more shallow.*

Hood House. It stretched southwards from Robin Hood Lane to where the M2 now lies, and from the Peripheral Road in the west, to the parish boundary along Forest Drive and the lower end of Marlow Copse. Part of it was owned by the Corrall family, 42 acres (17ha), and the rest by Mr T F Best, 69 acres (28ha). Impton complies with Hasted's positioning of Eccles "at the eastern extremity of the parish". The North Wood/Gredhurst site would position it by the northern boundary.

There is some evidence that Impton has not always been woodland. There was a pond in Corrall's portion of Impton (*Plate 19*). It is shown on the Tithe Map and survived until development took place in the 1970s; it now lies under the gardens of Nos 1 and 2 Tavistock Close. The large oak tree which stood in the front garden of No 2 grew at the edge of the pond. Immediately east of it was a hollow-way leading towards the valley, its banks covered with a rich growth of mosses and young ferns. It extended to a point level with the line of trees which now stand in front of Nos. 89–105 Woodbury Road. A path lay in it, but I know of no tradition that it was ever a right-of-way. The hollow-way may well have been a boundary ditch; it approximated to the boundary between Mr Best's and Mr Corrall's portions of Impton. Also within Impton are abrupt changes in level, usually about two feet (60cm), which may be old hedge-banks. Anyone who has walked through the woods to the tunnel under the motorway, will have crossed one of them. Another runs through my own garden. Pond, hollow-way and hedge-banks are more characteristic of farmland than of woodland, suggesting that they are the relics of an older landscape.

Further evidence of earlier cultivation of Impton was drawn to my attention by my neighbours. Their house was built in 1961. To my knowledge, the site had been wooded since the 1930s, and prior to this, the maps indicate woodland since at least 1801. It was chestnut coppice and the stubs were large ones. Indeed, when the site was being cleared for building, after two days the contractor retreated in confusion, his heavy plant broken, while the chestnut stubs remained triumphantly in position. Yet, when my neighbours eventually began to work their garden, they noticed that there were no large flints in the top layers, though plenty further down. This suggests that the land had, at some time, been in cultivation for a sufficiently long time for the flints to be weathered into smaller ones, or collected and removed.

Some documentary evidence supports the hypothesis that Impton was part of Eccles manor. Hasted informs us that during the 17th century the manor was held by the Sedleys, and that it was they who fragmented it, as outlined at the beginning of this Chapter. The estate papers of the Best family include accounts for tree-felling during the early decades of the 18th century.[3] With the accounts for the earliest years, 1707–1719, is correspondence showing that Thos. Best negotiated the purchase of woodland from Sir Chas Sedley. The total list of woods is extensive, but the only ones which lie in Aylesford parish are Gredhurst, Impton, Tottington (thus spelled, though in later papers it changes to Tappenden), Kite Hill and Hurst Hill. All of these, except Impton, lie at the northern edge of the parish. Only Impton lies at the "eastern extremity".

The earliest accounts give a total acreage for Impton of 23 acres (9.3ha). Slightly later ones, 1723–1736, refer to Great Impton, 18 acres (7.3ha), and Little Impton, seven acres (2.8ha). This suggests that only part of the area was wooded, though the figures need to be treated with caution, as they refer to the areas felled, not necessarily to the total areas of woodland. As indicated above, by 1841 Mr Best's portion of Impton Wood amounted to 69 acres. There was large-scale planting of woodland in north Kent during the 18th century. Deliberate planting of arable or meadow-land in Impton would conform to this pattern.

The areas of the other woods also increased from a total of 64 acres (27.9ha), as given on the wood-felling accounts between 1707–1719, to 110 acres (44.5ha) in 1841, though the same caution applies as to Impton. The trees planted were mostly sweet chestnut, with some oak and ash. Much of the chestnut was for hop-poles. Hop growing began in Kent about AD 1600. In the early years, every hop plant was given its own pole; the use of twine to support the plants was a later innovation.

Unexpected support for the hypothesis that Impton was once a settlement is provided by Richardson.[4] In his *Local Historian's Encyclopaedia*, he quotes a list of charters granting Markets and Fairs, issued by the Government in 1889, but said to be based on an earlier manuscript. Included in the list for Kent is a market and fair at 'Impeton'. I know of no place in Kent with a name like this, even allowing for the changes which occur in place-names over the centuries. The only other *Imp-* name is Impkins, near Charing, which seems never to have had a *-ton* ending.[5] Unless 'Impeton' can be positively identified as being elsewhere, it would seem a reasonable assumption that it was, in fact, Impton. Richardson also states that older sites of both markets and fairs may be on hill-tops or at boundaries. Impton is both (though see also the next Chapter). It lies on a hill overlooking Walderslade Valley. In terms of parishes, it lies at the junction of Aylesford, Boxley and Chatham. In terms of manors, it adjoins both Boxley and Walderslade manors.

The charter for a market and fair at 'Impeton' was granted by Edward I in the 29th year of his reign (AD 1300). If my hypothesis is correct then, in 1300, there was a thriving community in the north-eastern corner of what is now Aylesford parish. If it was, indeed, Eccles manor, it explains the group of names in the area which end in *-ton*, such as Impton, Taddington, Fostington and Yatterton, all shown on the Tithe Assessment. The ending *-ton* was Jutish for a farm or manor. The names are inexplicable if the area has always been woodland, but make sense if it was farmland which was later planted with trees, or allowed to revert to woodland. The presence of a manorial holding in the area would also explain why Aylesford parish later became responsible for two lengths of the Roman Road, as mentioned in Chapter One. Before 1555, upkeep of the roads was a manorial responsibility. We would, therefore, expect Impton/Eccles to be allocated a stretch of road to maintain. This may have been the length between the parish boundary north of Bridgewood Cottage and the boundary with Chatham.

The first part of the name, *Imp-*, could be derived from a personal name, as in Impkins,[5] or it could be an Anglo-Saxon word which, according to Harvey, meant a graft, scion, young shoot or sapling.[6] Stamper, quoting Harvey, refers to the field names 'impyard' and 'impgarth', found from the early 12th to the 15th centuries.[7] These contained trees, though it is not clear whether they were tree nurseries or plantations of young trees. This derivation would be quite appropriate to our Impton which, to this day, grows trees better than it grows anything else. There is also a similarity of meaning between Impton, interpreted as a farm where trees grow, and Eccles, meaning Oak Meadow.[5] Of the other three -*ton* names, I offer no explanation, except to say that they may have been derived from personal names and that the tree-felling accounts from 1707 to 1710 refer to Tottington, not Taddington. If the land, comprising the manor of Impton/Eccles, was divided between the top of the hill and the fertile land at the foot of the downs, it seems possible that the manor of Tottington was similarly split. It is increasingly recognised that manors were not necessarily compact land holdings, but could include blocks of land, separated by considerable distances.

If the hypothesis is correct, we can speculate as to the position of the centre of the manor. The obvious choice is Robin Hood House. The older name for this, shown on the 1819 Ordnance Survey map, was Borlin. This could well be Jutish, from *bor*, meaning high or elevated, and *hlinc*, meaning a bank, ridge or rising ground, though in the absence of earlier records we cannot be certain of it. In 1841, there were two ponds in the farmyard; Robin Hood Lane ran directly to and through the middle of the farmyard. Mr Anthony Mackay-Miller, who lived in the house at one time, considers that part of the present house dates from at least Tudor times. As mentioned in Chapter Three, it is one of the farms at the parish boundary, which could imply that its position predates the boundary.

Finally, to return to Hasted, with whom we started this Chapter. He informs us that Mr Best's part of Eccles manor seems "to have been made liable to payment of castle guard rent for the whole of it to Rochester Castle". So, all you good people of Tavistock Close, and Catkin and Sheraton and Tunbury and Marlow Copse and Forest Drive, etc, be prepared. If Rochester Castle is attacked, you're all liable to do guard duty!

Chapter Six — References
Where Was Eccles?

1) Hasted, E, **History of Kent**, Vol IV. Published 1778–1801. Reprinted 1972, by EP Publishing Ltd, in collaboration with Kent County Library.
2) CTR 12B Kent Archives Office. Tithe Map of Aylesford Parish. CTR 12A Kent Archives Office. Tithe Assessments for Aylesford Parish.
3) U480/E49 Estate Papers of the Best Family.
4) Richardson, J, **The Local Historian's Encyclopaedia**, Entry R11. Published by Historical Publications Ltd, 54 Station Road, New Barnet, Hertfordshire, 1974.
5) Glover, J, **Place-names of Kent**.
6) Harvey, J, **Early Nurserymen**. Published 1974, Chichester Press.
7) Grenville Astill and Annie Grant (Editors), **The Countryside of Mediaeval England**, pp 135–136. Published 1988 by Basil Blackwell Ltd.

Chapter Seven
Jack Barling's Meadows

Behind the Medway Crematorium lies a group of quiet meadows, known for most of this century as Jack Barling's Meadows. Warren Road lies along their western edge, and woods enclose them on the other three sides. At first glance they seem to have no historical interest, but they repay further consideration.

Two indentures, of 1786 and 1806, quote an earlier one of 1779, which refers to the meadows by field-names which have now fallen out of use, including the Ladyland, Farnham Croft and Heathy Field.[1,2] The indentures have no map or plan, but by comparing the areas of the fields, and with the help of sundry descriptive details, I have attempted to match the old names with the divisions of the meadows as shown on the Tithe Map (see *Table 1* and *Map 5*). I had tentatively assigned Farnham Croft to the eastern edge of the meadows, when unexpected support was supplied by a planning application to fell the adjacent woods.[3] The map which accompanied the application included the name Farnham Wood in brackets after the name Frith Wood, thus locating it east of the meadows, though perhaps not quite in the correct place. As written, it suggest that Farnham Wood was an alternative name for Frith, whereas they were two separate woods. Frith is shown in the Tithe Assessment as having an area of 103 acres (41.7ha). A twenty-year lease for Fern Ham Wood, dated 1778, gives its area as forty acres (16.2ha).[4] I suggest that this may be Tithe Map parcel number 634 (see Map 5), which had an area of thirty acres, and lay immediately east of the meadows, adjacent the parcels which seem to constitute Farnham Croft. The term *croft* referred to arable or meadow land adjacent to a house, rather like a small-holding. As late as 1841, the Tithe Map showed a house at the north-eastern corner of the meadows, where a small piece of waste land juts out from the woods and where, as some people will remember, an old lady lived in a caravan during the 1950s.

Farnham is an old settlement. The 16th century historian William Lambarde toured Kent, and in 1570 published an account of his

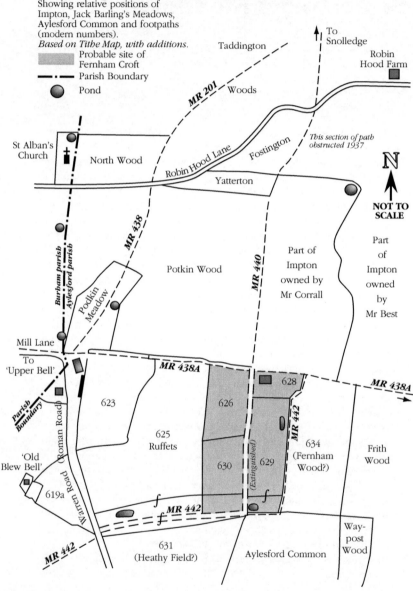

Map 5
Jack Barling's Meadows and Fernham Croft
Showing relative positions of
Impton, Jack Barling's Meadows,
Aylesford Common and footpaths
(modern numbers).
Based on Tithe Map, with additions.

Probable site of
Fernham Croft

— ·— Parish Boundary

● Pond

Taddington

To
Snolledge

Robin
Hood Farm

MR 201   Woods

St Alban's
Church

North Wood

Robin Hood Lane

Fostington

This section of path
obstructed 1937

N

NOT TO
SCALE

Yatterton

Burbam parish
Aylesford parish

MR 438

Potkin Wood

MR 440

Part of
Impton
owned by
Mr Corrall

Part
of
Impton
owned
by
Mr Best

Podkin
Meadow

Mill Lane
To
'Upper Bell'

MR 438A

MR 438A

Parish
Boundary

Roman Road

623

MR 442

626

628

634
(Fernham
Wood?)

Frith
Wood

625
Ruffets

'Old
Blew Bell'

619a

630

(Extinguished)

629

Warren Road

MR 442

631
(Heathy Field?)

Aylesford Common

Way-
post
Wood

70

Table 1

Suggested correlation between names of fields (Jack Barling's Meadows) as given on an indenture of 1779, quoted in another of 1806, and names and numbers on Tithe Map of 1843

Description/name as given in the Indentures (Note: All areas given as *n* acres [hectares] "more or less")	Number on Map	Name	Area Acres/Rods/Perches [hectare]
6± acres [2.4ha] adjoining to a certain wood called Potkin Wood and to Burham Common	644	Potkin (= Podkin Meadow)	6.0.25 [2.5ha]
4± acres [1.6ha] adjoining to the Barn aforesaid	623	Barn	4.0.1 [1.6ha]
16± acres [6.5ha] 1786 … Rough land or wood 1806 … Piece or parcel of rough ground called the Ladyland	625	Ruffet (Wood)	17.0.11 [6.9ha]
4± acres [1.6ha] One piece or parcel of land adjoining the Ladyland and Aylesford Common	—	Wood at southern edge, tied to Ruffets	—
2½± acres [1ha] Adjoining the house (= "The Blue Bell")	619a	Old Bell	1.2.15 [0.6ha]
4± acres [1.6ha] called Heathy Field. In 1786 it was described as "now planted with ash".	631	Ash Plantation	5.1.9 [2.15ha]
Farnham Croft:			
1779 "3 pieces or parcels of land in 4 pieces commonly called or known … as … Farnham Croft and a little orchard there-unto adjoining with the appurtenances containing 4± acres [1.6ha] and all those two messuages or tenements and one barn and other outhouses and buildings there-unto belonging then standing and being on the last-mentioned 5 pieces.	628 626 630 629	House and garden Four acres Three acres Long Meadow	0.1.31 [0.2ha] 3.2.31 [1.5ha] 2.2.37 [1.1ha] 3.1.31 [1.4ha]
1786 As above but total area corrected to 9± acres [3.6ha].			

(1 acre = 0.4ha; 1 rod or rood = 0.25 acre = 0.1ha; 1 perch = 30¼ square yards = 25.29m² = 0.0025ha.)

"perambulations".[5] When he writes about Aylesford parish he digresses to describe how, in AD 893, Danes invaded the Thames Estuary in eighty ships. Some camped in Essex, while the others camped at "Middleton", usually interpreted as Milton-next-Sittingbourne. Another contingent had arrived on the south coast, near Winchelsea (the *Anglo-Saxon Chronicle* says Appledore).[6] From these bases they sent out raiding parties. To use Lambarde's words: "[They] spoilet the countrie in sundrie partes at once …". Kent by this time had ceased to be a kingdom in its own right, and had been annexed to Wessex, which was governed by King Alfred — he who burnt the cakes. He was a much better soldier and king than he was a cook. He first gained control of London, so that the Danes could not sail up the Thames and penetrate into the heart of England, as they had done on previous occasions. He then stationed his troops in a strategic position, halfway between the Danes in the Thames Estuary and those on the south coast. After about a year, the latter moved north to join those in Essex. Alfred's troops out-rode the Danes. Where they rode from is not clear (one writer considers that the half-way point was Charing Heath)[7] but on one point Lambarde is quite specific: "When they came at a place in this parish called, both now and anciently, Fernham, that is, the ferny town or dwelling, one part of the King's power couragiously charged them, and finding them given to flight, followed the chase upon them so fiercely that they were compelled to take the Thamise without boat or bridge, in which passage there were a great number of them drowned, the residue having enough to do to save their own lives and to convey over their Capitaine, that had a deadly wound."

The Anglo-Saxons in this campaign were led by Edward, Alfred's son and successor, and his brother-in-law, Ethelred. The Danes' overall commander was the formidable Haesten, who had turned his attention to south-east England, after being repulsed on the continent.[8] The two-pronged attack, from the estuary and the south coast, seems to have been designed as a pincer movement to gain control of Kent. It failed, and although the Danes continued raiding for another 160 years, they never again launched an attack on the scale of Haesten's grand strategy. The Dane-law was established in the north, and extended down the east coast from York to Essex, but Kent remained under the control of the Anglo-Saxons. It would seem that one of the decisive battle in determining this was fought in Jack Barling's quiet meadows.

The indenture of 1779, referred to above, includes Podkin Meadow, though it does not use the name, referring to it merely as six acres (2.4ha) of land lying between Potkin Wood and Burham Common. In the late 1940s a line resembling an old hedge-bank was visible across the meadow, dividing it into two approximately equal portions, which suggests that Podkin was originally two fields. This must have been prior to 1779, as the area at that date was given as six acres (2.4ha), which it still is. The apparent division was accompanied by a number of 'fairy rings' lying on either side of it, suggesting that there were old tree roots under the ground, which were slowly rotting down. The presence of the division was confirmed in the autumn of 1988, when the meadow was ploughed for the first time in living memory. Typically, soil on the Hill is brown and liberally strewn with flints of all sizes. Its texture varies from that of soggy dough, to that of brick, depending on the weather. In Podkin, the soil was black; black as peat and with almost as fine a tilth. A few small stones were scattered on the surface. Where the division had been visible in the 1940s, was a line of our usual orange-brown clay, complete with massive flints. Without going into the technicalities of soil profiles and their classification, we can, perhaps, note that soils with a very deep, humous-rich top layer are characteristic of natural grassland, such as the North American prairies and the Russian steppes[9]. Podkin is not natural grassland, because no part of the British Isles is natural grassland, but the soil suggest that it has been maintained as grassland by humans and their animals for a long, long time — long enough for it to have acquired the characteristic soil of natural grassland.

We turn now to the Ladyland. In 1779, the estimated area of this was 16 acres (6.5ha). I have equated it with the Tithe Map parcel called Ruffets. The Ladyland was described in 1786 as rough land or wood, and in 1806 simply as rough land. It is easy to see how, by 1841, this had become Ruffets. It has the shape of a reversed capital 'L', the stem forming the central part of the meadows, and the foot extending westwards to Warren Road. Its 17 acres (6.9ha) amount to nearly half the total area of the meadows. The 1819 Ordnance Survey map shows it as woodland separating two non-wooded areas, one adjacent to Warren Road, and the other being Farnham Croft (see *Table 1* and *Map 5*). In the absence of earlier records, we can only speculate on the origin of the name, but I put forward three suggestions;

1.   It may, at one time, have been owned or tenanted by a lady. I shall return to this possibility later in the Chapter.

2.   The name is sometimes given to land belonging to a church dedicated to the Blessed Virgin Mary. Eccles manor is believed to have had a church. Indeed, some authorities derive its name from Aiglessa, meaning a church, though Glover derives

it from *ac*, meaning oak, and *leys*, meaning meadows.[10] If Eccles did have a church, and if Eccles and Impton were part of the same manor, where was the church situated? Was it near modern Eccles, or should we be looking for it somewhere near Impton? Was there, perhaps, a wayside chapel near Warren Road?

3. The third suggestion is that Ladyland is a corruption of Ladeland, from the old English *lade*, meaning a way or path. Our terms laden and bill of lading have the same origin, indicating preparation for sending goods along a 'way'. Is it merely coincidence that there is a Lade Field at the top of Detling Hill, in a similar position to our Ladyland, at the boundary between Detling and Thurnham?[11]

If we look at the meadows and the 'ways' serving them we find that a large number of paths converge on them. The Roman Road lies along their western edge. The meadows, even to this day, are surrounded on their other three sides by footpaths. The Upper Green Way, across Burham Common, led to their north-western corner. Prior to 1988, the parish boundary between Aylesford and Burham ran straight up the hill to this corner, suggesting that it had been a local reference point for many years. From this same corner, the path across Podkin Meadow strikes off in a north-easterly direction. The path from Kits Coty joins the Roman Road at the south-western corner of the meadows. A track across Aylesford Common joined them half-way along their southern edge. This track continued straight across the meadows to Fernham Croft in the north-eastern corner: it is still traceable on the ground, though the modern footpath has diverged from it, and skirts the edge of the meadows. From this same north-eastern corner, two paths diverge — FP 438A runs due east through the woods to Cossington Fields Farm, heading towards Westfield Sole, and thence to Lidsing and Bredhurst, while FP 440 leads into the valley which eventually crosses Robin Hood Lane, widens to form Taddington Valley, and hence to Snolledge Bottom.

If Impton was a manor, and if it was the Impeton included by Richardson in his list of Markets and Fairs, then Impton had a fair. Markets were usually held weekly. It seems unlikely that they would be held on demesne land, as the continual trampling would render it unsuitable for cultivation. Jack Barling's meadows are adjacent to Impton (see *Map 5*). Like Impton itself, they lie at the top of a hill. Also, like Impton, they lie at a boundary — that between Aylesford and Burham. And all tracks converged on them. Further, Richardson indicates that market and fair sites were often situated at the junction of old tracks or drove roads.[12] Old tracks? The Roman Road lies beside the meadows; the Upper Green Way, possibly of Bronze Age origin (see Chapter Eight) leads to them. Footpaths 438A and 440 formed the boundaries between Impton and other parcels of land with equally old names, such as Fostington, Yatterton and Frith, suggesting that these paths date back to at least Jutish times. All old tracks, indeed.

The meadows occupy a gap in the pattern of common land. On the chalk slope, below the 'Upper Bell', there is evidence that common land was originally continuous from Wouldham to the 'Lower Bell'. Burham Common, which we have already seen extended on both sides of the Upper Green Way, reached the edge of Podkin Meadow.[1,2] Aylesford Common abutted the southern edge of the meadows. We might, therefore, have expected the meadows themselves to be common land. Richardson states that markets and fairs were often on ancient sites, and that charters of the middle ages merely regularised them, and granted the revenues to local land-owners. Was this, perhaps, the origin of Jack Barling's meadows? Was it an ancient market site, held originally on common land? Did the charter of 1300 effectively enclose this common land? Hasted records that during the reign of Edward I (1272–1307), Richard de Rokesle (Ruxley) held the manor of Eccles as "half a knight's fee of Margery Rivers as she did of Warine de Montchensie".[13] Prior to AD 1400, this seems to have been the only difference between the manors of Eccles and Tottington. Was this how the Lady-land acquired its name? Did the granting of the charter for a market and fair effectively increase Richard of Ruxley's salary in line with inflation? Did the 'Old Blew Bell' originate as the house providing shelter and refreshment for the officials who were present to collect tolls from the traders and to rule on any disputes regarding weights and measures? Trading was permitted only within certain hours. Was it from the 'Old Blew Bell' that the bell was rung to mark the beginning and end of trading?

We do not know. We shall probably never know. But, when you walk the path through the meadows, remember that you walk on ancient ground. Listen carefully. Hidden in the muted roar of motorway traffic may be ghostly echoes of long-ago traders calling their wares. The ferns growing at the foot of trees in the near-by woods are direct descendants of those which gave the ancient settlement of Fernham its name. And on bright summer days, when white horse-daisies gleam from edge to edge of the fields, and the red sorrel dances between, spare a thought for the men of both sides who, loyal to their leaders and their companions, fought and died in Jack Barling's quiet meadows 1,100 years ago.

Chapter Seven — Appendix
Location of Farnham

The Anglo-Saxon Chronicle refers to the battle of Farnham without locating it exactly. Some modern writers interpret it as Farnham in Surrey. I prefer to follow Lambarde, and interpret it as Farnham in Aylesford, for the following reasons:

1. The oral tradition was still strong when Lambarde was writing, and may have reinforced his interpretation.

2. Although the meaning of the Anglo-Saxon Chronicle is often ambiguous, its account of this particular episode makes it clear that the Danes, who had camped at Appledore, were heading for Essex to join the rest of the Danish army. I find it difficult to believe that they would have detoured to Farnham in Surrey. From the south coast, they could have used Stone Street, running northwards from Hythe, but they would then have risked a major confrontation at Canterbury. Alternatively, they could have travelled westwards until they had passed Winchelsea, and then headed north along what is now the A229. This route avoided major towns. At its northern end, in the vicinity of Blue Bell Hill, it offered a choice between veering north-eastwards to the Danish base at Milton, or north-westwards towards the stretch of river between Higham and Rochester. It is believed that river crossings existed in this area in Roman times, when the sea level was lower, and the estuary probably did not extend further upstream than Cliffe. During the next few centuries, the sea level rose (or the land sank), and the estuary extended further upstream, but some of the crossing may still have existed in AD 894.

3. It is possible that many writers do not know of the existence of Farnham in Aylesford. Even the Kentish antiquary Beale-Poste, writing in the middle of the 19th century, did not know of its location, though he knew of its existence. In modern terms, it is a non-place. Modern writers, especially those from outside Kent, may assume it to be Farnham in Surrey because they are not aware of the other possibility.

Chapter Seven — References
Jack Barling's Meadows

1) U896/T5 Kent Archives Office. Indenture of 1786.
2) U896/T5 Kent Archives Office. Indenture of Lease and Release, 9th April 1806.
3) TR/100/86 Planning application to fell woodland, submitted to Tonbridge & Malling Council, 18th December 1986.
4) U229/T4 Kent Archives Office. Lease, dated 16th October 1778.
5) Lambarde, W, **A Perambulation of Kent**. Published 1570.
6) **Anglo-Saxon Chronicle**. (Compiled) Edited by J A Giles. Published 1907 by George Ball & Sons.
7) Blaxland, Gregory, **South-Eastern England, Eternal Battleground**. Published by Meresborough Books, Rainham, 1981.
8) Woodruff, Douglas, **Life and Times of Alfred the Great**. Published by Weidenfeld & Nicolson, 1974.
9) Hall, Daniel, **The Soil**, pp 26–28 and 272–273. Published by J Murray, 5th Edition, 1945.
10) Glover, Judith, **The Place-names of Kent**. Published by Meresborough Books, Rainham, 1982.
11) U588/P1 Kent Archives Office. Map of the Demesne Land of Manor of Thurnham.
12) Richardson, J, **The Local Historian's Encyclopaedia**, Ref R2. Published by Historical Publications Ltd, New Barnet, Hertfordshire.
13) Hasted, E, **History of Kent**, Vol. IV.

Chapter Eight
The Chalk Pits

Chalk has been dug from the Downs for many years. The parish church of All Saints in Wouldham, dating from AD 1258, has two pillars made of chalk blocks. Great Culand Farmhouse, which had the date 1592 over the doorway, was partly built of chalk. Chalk is not the best of building materials. The expertise required to use it is unlikely to have been acquired from one or two isolated occasions; rather, it suggests steady experience of handling the material. On the boundary between Wouldham and Burham lies Scarborough Farm. The name, which is Anglo-Saxon in origin, is interpreted by Glover as meaning 'a stronghold by a cleft or gap'.[1] If the cleft, or scar, refers to a chalk-pit it must have been there in Jutish times when the name originated, though we must remember that chalk-pits are not the only cause of scarring. The most prominent scars on Blue Bell Hill today are the great cliffs resulting from the construction of the new A229 in the 1970s.

The use of chalk or lime as an agricultural dressing was well-known by the 17th century. Some was dug from chalk banks, and some from holes which were literally pits. According to a talk on dene-holes, given to Rochester Natural History Society in 1886, these had been used to provide lime for agricultural purposes "within living memory"; it was easier to dig down than to carry the chalk long distances over badly-surfaced roads.[2] By the 18th century, lime-burning was well established. Lime was lighter to transport than chalk, and had a wider range of uses, including the making of mortar, which was becoming increasingly important with the burgeoning use of brick as a building material. Pits were still small, mostly supplying just a single kiln.

This was the origin of the pits on Blue Bell Hill, later to become Sandford's Lime Works. Eventually, there would be three pits. The earliest was the most northerly of the three, lying to the east of the Turnpike Road (Old Chatham Road), just south of the modern footbridge. It was already in existence in 1841.[3.1] It was during the 1840s that Mr Sandford's great-grandfather came from London as a young man to run the quarry for his aunt, Mrs Polly Oliver.[4] According to a lease of 1871, Thomas Oliver was landlord of the Kits Coty Beer-house.[3.2] Chalk-quarrying and beer went together: quarrying was thirsty work, and so was lime-burning. Pubs and ale-houses prolifer-ated near the quarries. In north Kent, Swanscombe is usually credited with having the greatest number of pubs per head of population, but Burham in its heyday probably ran it a close second.

When Mr Sandford's great-grandfather died in 1894, his two sons took over the lime-works.[4] By this time, there were two more pits, one on either side of Kits Coty House. During the 1890s, the two brothers purchased all the land between the old A229 and Warren Road. Mr Sandford has, in his possession, an interesting drawing of Kits Coty monument showing, as usual, Kits Coty House in the background, but with a complete line of chalk cliff behind it, and extending to left and right of it. Presumably this represents an early stage in the devel-opment of the two southern pits. The Enclosure Award for Aylesford Common provided for the retention of a footpath on the hill above Kits Coty House, to be known as Chalk Cliff Path.[3.3] The drawing illus-trates the aptness of the name. Quarrying continued into the 1970s, and markedly changed the contours of the land in this corner of the Downs, partly by the quarrying itself, and partly by the depositing of spoil and consequent regrading of areas already quarried. In the 1970s, there was a final flurry of activity as the quarry was extended to coincide with the 'cut' required by KCC Highways Department for the construction of the new A229. The three pits are now occupied by Lower Bell Industrial Estate.

Unlike most pits in the Medway Gap, those on Blue Bell Hill never supplied chalk for the cement industry. When the reports were compiled for the KCC's first Mineral Subject Plan, Sandford's Lime-works was the only remaining lime-works in the county. The uses made of lime over the life of the pits were many and varied. In addition to its agricultural use, it was used for plastering and lime-washing. The latter was much used in the 19th and early 20th centuries as a form of cheap distemper-cum-mild-disinfectant; it was applied indiscriminately to cowsheds and chicken houses, sculleries and kitchens. Lime was used by the sewage works at Aylesford and Motney Hill. It was bought by Williamson's Tanning Works at Canterbury, where it was used to emulsify the layer of fat immediately under the hides. It was used by Chatham laundries to soften water. This procedure was possible only where the hardness was 'temporary', in other words caused by calcium bicarbonate. The amount of lime had to be calculated carefully, as too much would remove the temporary hardness but replace it by permanent hardness. Consequently it was used only where large volumes of water were being treated, such as in laundries. Possibly the most macabre use of the lime was by Maidstone Prison Authority for disposing of the bodies of prisoners who had been executed, and who, under a quirk of ancient history, were denied decent burial in a churchyard.[4]

At the peak of their activity, there were twelve kilns operating in the Blue Bell Hill lime-works. Nine of these were flare kilns, and three were tunnel or bottle kilns. Mr. Sandford provided the following description of the flare kilns.

The walls, which were made of brick and lined with firebricks, were 15in (38cm) thick. Inside the front entrance were grids, approximately 2ft

Figure 1 – Lime Burning
Diagrammatic Section through a Flare Kiln

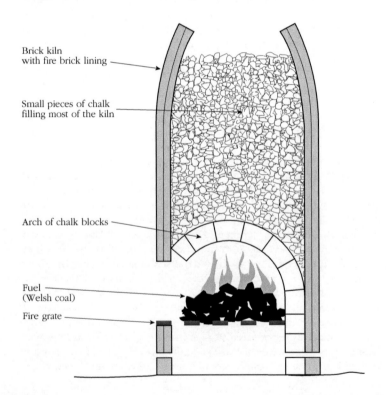

Brick kiln
with fire brick lining

Small pieces of chalk
filling most of the kiln

Arch of chalk blocks

Fuel
(Welsh coal)

Fire grate

6in (75cm) off the ground. An arch of solid chalk blocks was built inside the kiln, just behind the entrance, then it was filled with smaller pieces up to the level of a side door. Welsh coal was placed on the grids, and the kiln fired (see *Figure 1*). It burned for three days and nights, sending flames 100ft (30m) into the air. At the onset of war in 1939, the use of these kilns had to be discontinued: the flames would have provided an excellent navigation beacon to enemy bombers seeking the nearby airfields of Detling, West Malling and Rochester. The tunnel kilns continued in use; these were fitted with griddles at the base through which the lime could be raked at intervals until the rakers drew fire. The whole kiln was filled with alternating layers of coke (1in (2.5cm)) and chalk (4in (10cm)) and could be replenished from an upper door. Even these had to be covered with corrugated iron to ensure that no glow emanated to guide enemy 'planes: black-out regulations were rigorously enforced in England's 'Bomb Alley',

A side-product of chalk-quarrying is flint. This varies in quantity according to the particular stratum of chalk, being particularly prevalent in the upper chalk. Flint from the Blue Bell Hill works was sold to the Staffordshire potteries. This was fairly regular practice in north Kent. Large quantities of flints from the great pits at Northfleet were tipped into the disused and flooded Blue Lake Pit, until Associated Portland Cement Manufacturers discovered that there was a market for them, when they promptly dredged them up again and sold them. There seems to have been some expertise in using flint as a building material. Minor examples of this still exist, for example the side wall of the outhouses at the Lower Bell, and a decorative tract in the wall of Blue Bell Hill chapel (see Plate 8). Two flint cottages survived into the 1930s between Robin Hood Lane and the newspaper shop. One of these may have been the 'wayside cottage' where the young men from Zion Baptists held Sunday services during the years before the chapel was built. There is flint-work in the garden wall of 'Fairview', Common Road, though Mrs Taylor, the occupier, informs me that some of this is modern[5]. If we travel a couple of miles eastwards, we find considerable examples of flint-work at Lidsing, Bredhurst, Kemsley Street and Guildstead. It would be interesting to know whether this developed as a side-line to chalk quarrying, or whether it represents an older tradition. Flint-working is, after all, the oldest of all crafts. The men who built Kits Coty monument were experts at it.

By modern standards, Blue Bell Hill pits are small. More conspicuous are the two Great Culand pits, immediately north of Eccles. These served Burham Cement Works, which originated as a brick-works in 1852, but by 1871 had diversified to become Burham Brick, Lime and Cement Co Ltd.[6.1] About this time, they acquired Culand Farm, and began to quarry the rough grazing which had originally been common land. The Ordnance Survey map of 1865 gives no indication of pit, but that of 1898 shows the older of the two pits well established. It occupied the field shown on the Tithe Map as Great Combe Field; it must have been an attractive stretch of downland prior to being quarried. Chalk was taken directly to the works by a narrow gauge railway, which ran — probably still lies — under the arable field south of the pit. Until recently, one of its air shafts was visible in the field as a small fenced enclosure, while the stile on the nearby path (FP 26) was partly constructed of lengths of old railway line. This quarry provided a large number of fossils, many of which found their way to the Geological Museum in London, where they helped to form the 'type series' for determining the stratigraphy of the chalk. Quarrying was carried out manually at that time; the workmen were able to see, collect and report geological and archeological artefacts. The mechanical excavators of today have neither the eyes to see them, nor the brains to recognise them.

In 1900, 'The Combine' was set up. This was a consortium of cement manufacturers, later to develop into Associated Portland Cement Manufacturers (APCM), now Blue Circle. This consortium bought up many small local cement companies, or made working arrangements with them, and proceeded to 'rationalise' them.[6] Some were closed completely, with corresponding large scale unemployment among the workers. Burham Cement Works escaped closure, not because of any inherent advantage over the others — indeed, it was the wrong side of the river to make use of the railway as transport — but because O'Hagan, the driving force behind APCM at its inception, had mortgaged it as part of the negotiation to acquire the constituent parts of 'The Combine'. He was therefore obliged to keep it working so that his creditors did not foreclose on the mortgage. Thanks to this purely financial arrangement, we not only have the original Culand Pit, but also the rectangular one lying east of it, adjacent the Pilgrims' Way. Chalk was still being extracted from this in the 1930s. I can remember that, as a child, one of the minor excitements of a visit to Burham Downs was seeing the 'little trains' going into the tunnel under the road. Burham Works did not finally close until 1941.[6.2]

Coles-Finch, writing in the early 1920s, states "There is sure proof that the Romans and before them our ancestors lived in the vicinity of Kewland ... At the commencement of the excavation of the above-mentioned chalk quarry numerous human interments were found in conjunction with rare and perfect Roman pottery. These were handed to the authorities owning the works and lost to the general public!" It is not clear to which of the two Culand Pits he is referring, though from the date of his writing and consideration of the topography, I infer that it is the rectangular one. It seems possible that this was the cemetery which served the enormous Roman villa at Eccles, scarcely a mile to the south, which Detsicas was unable to find when he excavated the villa during the 1970s.[8]

Culand, also spelt Kewland, is first mentioned in 1254, but the name is Anglo-Saxon, meaning *Cuda's Land*.[1] The farm was supplied with water from a well nearly 200ft deep (61m), from which water was raised by a treadmill now at Maidstone Museum, visible from the outside if you walk through Brenchley Gardens.[9] We can speculate whether this well was Roman. The Romans are known to have dug deep wells, often for the purpose of supplying water to their flocks and herds.[10] Great Culand Farmhouse is gone forever, demolished in 1953. Its remains are visibly scattered over the field to the west of the track between the two pits (FP 24). The two pits, together with some of the downland above them, now form part of the Burham Site of Special Scientific Interest (SSSI), which is held by the Kent Trust for Nature Conservation on a lease from APCM which expires in 1999; the pits form the last refuge for plants and insects which were once common on the downs and along the Pilgrims' Way. Long may they continue to do so.

Chapter Eight — References
The Chalk Pits

1)   Glover, Judith, **The Place-names of Kent**
2)   Proceedings of the Rochester Natural History Society, Vol I, p 265
     Talk by Chas Bird, BA, FGS, on 'Rochester Dene-holes', 1886.
3)   Kent Archives Office
     3.1)   CTR 12B Tithe Map, Aylesford Parish.
     3.2)   U 1823/77 T2.2 Sundry Title Deeds from Maidstone
            Museum Collection.
     3.3)   Q/RDC/19 Enclosure Award, Aylesford Common.
4)   Oral Information: Mr P Sandford.
5)   Oral Information: Mrs P Taylor, Common Road.
6)   Preston, J, **Industrial Medway**. Published by J Preston,
     printed by W and J Mackay Ltd, 1977.
     6.1)   pp 93–94
     6.2)   pp 166–174
     6.3)   p 201
7)   Coles-Finch, W, **In Kentish Pilgrim Land**, p 37. Published 1925,
     by C W Daniel Co, Graham House, Tudor Street, London EC4.
8)   **Detsicas**, *Archeologia Cantania*, Vol XCII, 1976, p 163.
9)   Bergess W and Sage S, **Five Medway Villages**, p. 17.
     Published 1983, Meresborough Books, Rainham, Kent.
10) Birley, A, **Life in Roman Britain**, p 84. Published 1964, B T
     Batsford.

Chapter Nine

Kits Coty
and other Antiquities

No history of Blue Bell Hill would be complete without mention of the best-known antiquity in the area — Kits Coty House. The four great sarsen stones are the remains of a communal tomb of people who lived in the area some 4,000 years ago. 400 yards (365m) south of it lies Little Kits Coty, better known as the Countless Stones of Aylesford, which is the remains of another tomb destroyed in the 18th century. These are only two of an extensive group of burials which lie at the foot of the hill. The group includes the Coffin Stone, north of Great Tottington, under which two skulls were found, and Smythe's Megalith, south of Lower Warren Road, discovered in 1823, and of which nothing now remains. The White Horse Stone, adjacent the Pilgrims' Way, near the Aylesford/Boxley boundary, may be another; it is the second sarsen to bear this name. The original lay in the north-western angle of the junction between Pilgrims' Way and the Rochester/Maidstone Road, but was broken up in 1834.[1] Two sarsens lying in the same field as Smythe's Megalith were excavated by McCrerie in 1956; he suggested that they were the remains of another burial chamber, and could be "clearly seen set in a low east-west mound".[2] Two mounds can still be seen in this field by anyone standing on Lower Warren Road and looking southwards across the field. Yet another was discovered in 1980 when a local farmer hit it with his plough.[3] Kits Coty itself is the most northerly of the group, and stands on higher ground than the others. A survey in 1961 showed that the earthen mound which originally covered the stones still existed to a height of 3ft (0.9m); this mound is clearly visible in the well-known sketch of Kits Coty drawn about 1828. It was 200ft long (61m), and 30ft wide (9m); the 1961 survey revealed ditches lying along its northern and southern sides from which soil had been dug to make the mound.[3] It may have had a perilith (a fence of standing stones) or a stone curb. In the 18th century, Stukeley said that there was another stone to the north-west of it, which he called the General's Tombstone. This was partly destroyed in 1867, and its remains rediscovered in 1956.

The Neolithic, or New Stone Age, people who built Kits Coty were farmers and cattle-herders who arrived in England about 3,000 BC — some authorities say earlier.[4,5] They had no knowledge of metal or metal working. They are usually credited with clearing the forest from the Downs and the land to the south to obtain pasture and arable land. Pottery sherds, collected from Kits Coty Field, are late Neolithic, suggesting that the great megalithic tombs were not built until some centuries after they arrived. Philp dates the cemetery at the foot of the hill to the period 2,300–1,700 BC.[3] The building of such tombs pre-supposed a settled, well-organised community, which, by the standards of its time, was affluent. A community in which all the members were living at, or near, starvation level would be unlikely to have the time, energy or resources to carry out such major construction.

Howard Biggs, writing of the River Medway, states that "Aylesford … is the site of a very ancient and important crossing, a good shallow ford … the stones of Kits Coty stand alongside the old track leading up from the ford".[6] How old is the track, and where did it lead once it had passed Kits Coty? A modern footpath (MR 442) continues its line up the hill; this path is marked on the map of 1769, and is probably older. It emerges onto Warren Road opposite the south-western corner of Jack Barling's Meadows. At the eastern edge of these, scarcely five minutes' walk away and adjacent the suggested site of Fernham, is a shallow depression. This is the extreme tip of a dry chalk valley which leads to Luton. The upper end of the valley is now obscured by embankments of modern roads (M2, Peripheral Road), but it can be traced along MR 440 and the modern residential toad called Fernbank, then across Robin Hood Lane, where it becomes Taddington Valley. Below Fort Horsted, it turns through a sharp angle, and runs north-eastwards, past Snolledge Farm, and continues as Snolledge (Snodhurst) Bottom to Luton (See *Map 6*). It is known that the north Kent riverside from Chatham to Sittingbourne was extensively settled in Neolithic times; Luton valley formed part of this area[7]. When Fort Luton was constructed in 1891, a prehistoric burial was found overlooking the lower end of Snolledge Valley.[8] Presnail describes it in a section headed "Iron Age",[8] but the absence of any metal objects and the presence of a stag's antler — the typical Neolithic pick-axe — suggest an earlier date. Thus, the Snolledge–Taddington Valley lies between two areas of Neolithic settlement, and has a burial chamber at each end. Its whole length can be walked in two hours. Did it serve as a Neolithic route between the areas of settlement? If Kits Coty was a ceremonial site, did it serve just one settlement, or was it the venue

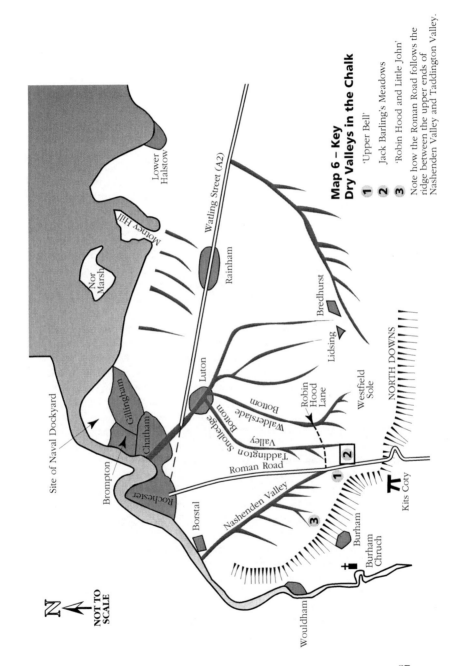

Map 6 – Key
Dry Valleys in the Chalk

1 'Upper Bell'

2 Jack Barling's Meadows

3 'Robin Hood and Little John'

Note how the Roman Road follows the ridge between the upper ends of Nashenden Valley and Taddington Valley.

for summit meetings between neighbouring tribes? We do not know, but it is a sobering thought that the quiet path through Impton and Taddington Woods may have been a public highway for 4,000 years, though it would be a mistake to think of it as a neat 6ft-wide path (1.8m). Neolithic routes were broad swathes of country which could be as much as a mile wide (1.6km).

The Neolithic tombs lie at the foot of the Downs. One of the Neolithic people's settlements has been discovered at the bottom of Blue Bell Hill by the archaeologists excavating in advance of the High Speed Rail Link. It was adjacent the path with starts opposite Warren Road and runs to Pilgrims Way, by the garage. Neolithic people also visited the top of the hill: their worked flints have been found at various locations. An early flint axe was found in the garden of No 1 Tavistock Close, adjacent the site of Impton Pond.[10] More recently, the occupier of a house along Mill Lane found three flint arrow heads in her garden. Was there, perhaps, a Stone Age workshop somewhere in the vicinity? Blue Bell Hill is high enough that the much-valued 'basal' layer of flint in the upper chalk had not been eroded away, and steep enough that it may have been exposed on the slope.[11,12]

Bronze Age people knew the top of the hill; Common Road may have originated as a Bronze Age track. Burham Enclosure Award refers to it as "The Upper Green Way lying near the brow of the hill".[13] This brow-of-the-hill position is said to be characteristic of Bronze Age tracks. At its western end, beyond the boundary with Wouldham, the track passes two Bronze Age burial mounds discovered in the early 1980s.[14] Cruse and Harrison, who excavated them, dated them to a period 1,800 to 1,400 BC. (For those interested, 1,800 BC was about the time that Abraham set out from Ur to go walk-about.) A third mound, perhaps better known, is the tump in Shoulder-of-Mutton Wood, above Lower Nashenden Farm. The Lower Medway Archeological Research Group excavated it some years ago and came to the conclusion that it was not prehistoric but the site of a mill. Below this stretch of the Downs lay the mediaeval Manor of Rings, still represented by Rings Hill Place and Rings Hill Farm. The name suggests that, in mediaeval times, a large number of circular Bronze Age mounds were visible, forming a complete burial ground. The route of the 'Upper Green Way' is further marked by a bronze axe, found in the garden of No 114 Common Road (*Plate 20*), and another at the northern edge of Podkin Meadow.[15] These scattered finds could indicate that our Bronze Age predecessors were regrettably careless, and left their tools lying around. On the other hand, they may have been left in houses which became unoccupied and eventually collapsed, burying the axes.

*Plate 20   Bronze axe and mineral nodules (probably pyrites) from the garden in
Common Road. Courtesy of Mrs Tanton.
(Photograph by Ronald White, Pudding Lane, Maidstone.)*

There is a tantalising possibility that a ceremonial site existed on
the hill, in either Neolithic times or Bronze Age, or both. In the first
half of the 19th century, the remains of a Roman building were found
along Warren Road. Further details will be given later in this chapter,
but one of the men who found and described it referred to it being
erected on a mound.[16] At about the same time, Mr Thomas Wright
was examining antiquities on the other side of the River Medway.
In his account, he states "In the south part of Addington parish are
several immense cones of earth, veritable pyramids, which have every
appearance of being artificial. The church of Addington is built on
one of them".[17] The last statement is indisputable. Addington church
is indeed built on a mound. If anyone doubts my word, go and have a
look at it! The church is a very short distance from the Chestnut Stones.
Thus, on one side of the river we have Neolithic burials (Chestnut
Stones, Coldrum Stones) and a church built on a mound. On the east

89

side we have Neolithic burials (Kits Coty, etc.) and a record of a Roman building situated on a mound. Moreover, the building is believed to have been a temple or other religious building.[18] Prehistoric mounds are known from other parts of the country; their function is unknown, but they are believed to have had some ceremonial or religious significance, and there is a strong tradition of invaders taking over religious sites of conquered peoples for their own religious purposes. It is also interesting in this connection that Coles-Finch (8c, pp 27–28) quotes Pryer (1861): "Flanking the Old Chatham Road lying eastwards of that now used, between the Upper and Lower Bell Inn and within quarter of a mile (400m) of Kits Coty House we saw, about 10 years since, a continuous avenue of greyweathers, some of them broken and thrown down but still preserving nearly their original position on either side of the way." Coles-Finch includes a sketch map which positions this avenue of stones at the upper end of Warren Road, approximating to the length of the road that has Jack Barling's Meadows on the east side and residential properties on the west. Avenues of standing stones are a well-known feature of Neolithic ceremonial sites.

The use of bronze was gradually superseded by the use of iron. About 600 BC there was an early Iron Age community near Aylesford

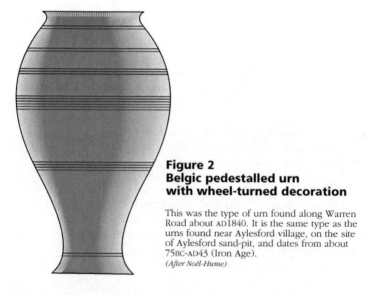

Figure 2
Belgic pedestalled urn
with wheel-turned decoration

This was the type of urn found along Warren Road about AD1840. It is the same type as the urns found near Aylesford village, on the site of Aylesford sand-pit, and dates from about 75BC-AD43 (Iron Age).
(After Noël-Hume)

village. Its cemetery, situated where Aylesford sand-pit now lies, was excavated in 1890, and judging by the articles found, it was a thriving and affluent society[19]. These early Iron Age residents buried their dead in distinctive pear-shaped urns mounted on small pedestals; the actual graves were flat, not mounded (*Figure 2*). A small number of these pedestalled urns were found on Blue Bell Hill, on or near the same site as the Roman building already mentioned.[18] It could be that a few residents of the Aylesford settlement were, for some obscure reason, buried on the hill instead of in the cemetery. On the other hand, the burials may indicate that there was an Iron Age farm on the hill. It will be suggested below that the urns were found in or near the southern borders of Jack Barling's meadows; again, we come across a hint that these meadows may have been farmland for a long time. Dare we speculate that they originated as an Iron Age farm?

The presence of Iron Age burials on the hill near the Roman Road supports the possibility that there was an Iron Age route down the hill before the Romans arrived. That brings us back to the Romans, with whom we started this book. As already mentioned, there was a Roman building on the hill. It was observed by two antiquaries in the 19th century — Messrs Charles and Wright. Wright's description is the more detailed.[17] He states that he "uncovered a few square yards of a floor of large bricks which had evidently been broken up and were mixed with what appeared to be roof tiles [and] with others which appeared like cornice mouldings. They were literally covered with broken pottery of every description, among which were several fragments of fine Samian ware mixed with a few human bones, some small nails and pieces of burnt wood". He deduced from this that the building had been destroyed by the 'barbarians' who invaded the country when the Romans left.

Despite such detailed descriptions from the 1830s and 1840s, no-one in the 20th century has been able to find it and its position is open to question. The Ordnance Survey Maps mark it on the brow of the hill above the old chalk-pits. This does not comply with Wright's account, which states that it was in a sheltered nook. Wright also states that it was just below Aylesford Common, whereas the Ordnance Survey Maps position it above part of the common. Anyone who has travelled down Blue Bell Hill may have noticed that the cliffs overlooking the A229 are divided by a steep, wooded combe, just north of the footbridge. If this is traced upwards, it emerges opposite Blue Bell Hill Farm. The tip of the combe could justifiably be described as a sheltered nook. The farm is immediately below that part of the common now occupied by Hazelwood Farm. Wright, in describing his excavations in 1844, indicated that pits full of flints were frequent in the vicinity of the ruins, though the pits had been raided as an easy supply of flints during the building of the Turnpike Road. Similar pits full of flints have recently been found during the excavations of a Roman building at Orpington. When the present owners of the house moved in, they found a surprising number of 'wells' in the vicinity of the house: were these, perhaps, the pits denuded of their flints? Against this background, I have suggested that the Roman building was not where the Ordnance Survey Maps mark it, but further up the road where Blue Bell Hill Farm now stands.[20] On the other hand, a visit by some experienced archaeologists gave no results — the scatter of debris associated with Roman ruins was not found. The site of Blue Bell Hill's Roman building remains a mystery.

Charles' account of the building is less detailed than Wright's. He was primarily interested in hoards of coins which he found in 1834.[16] These hoards were substantial, one of them containing more than 200 coins. The *Victoria County History*[18] refers to another hoard found in 1850. The coins ranged from those of Augustus (31 BC–AD 14) to Arcadius (AD 383–408), and thus cover the whole period of Roman occupation. It was Charles, also, who in 1842 reported the finding of "urns and other relics". He seems to have assumed that they were Roman, but it should be remembered that in 1842 the prehistoric succession from Stone Age through Bronze Age to Iron Age had not been identified, and views as to the length of time which elapsed prior to Greek and Roman times were vague. The Victoria County History, compiled in 1930, with the advantage of nearly 100 years of additional archaeological research, records no Roman urns, only the Iron Age ones referred to above.

Returning to Wright's account, he says that the building was "only a few hundred yards to the south of that on which Mr. Charles of Maidstone lately discovered a Roman burial ground. The cottagers ... tell me ... that the surface around this spot ... has never been disturbed by the plough". Two points of interest arise from this observation. Firstly, if I am correct in suggesting that the building was where Blue Bell Hill Farm now stands, then the coins and the [Iron Age] urns were found either in Jack Barling's Meadows, or in the belt of woodland along their southern border. The other point of interest relates to the name of Heathy Field, given in the indenture of 1779, and which I have equated with the Tithe Map entry number 631 (see Chapter Seven). This is the triangular patch of woodland immediately north of Blue Bell Hill Farm, adjacent Warren Road. Heathy Field is an unexpected name to find on the downs. Heaths are characteristic of sandy, acidic soils; typical heathland plants, such as heather and ling. do not grow wild on either the chalk or the thick, sticky clay-with-flints which overlies it. How, then, did it come by its name? There was an Anglo-Saxon place-name element: *snade* or *snoad* meaning detached land; detached, that is, in the legal sense rather than physically. Witney, in his fascinating book *The Jutish Forest*, makes out a case for this term gradually being corrupted to *hoath* and then rationalised into *heath*.[22] Further, he suggests that, originally, *snade* implied land which was detached because the king had kept it to himself. If I am correct in thinking that number 631 was Heathy Field, did it derive its name, long ago, from *snade* — the king's detached land? And, if so, why should the king have kept it? Was it because it was a burial ground? It was a superstitious age. Maybe the king did not want to risk stirring up ghosts. This would also explain why it was never ploughed. Or, had he found some of the hoards of coins and hoped to find some more? If the building was some sort of Roman temple, is this the explanation of the curiously Latin name Aiglessa, which some authorities consider to be the original name of Eccles?

Whether there was a Roman burial ground in the vicinity of Jack Barling's Meadows, or whether the burials were Iron Age, and the hoards of coins were hidden 500 years later when news arrived that "barbarians" were invading, remains uncertain. The undisputed Roman burials on the hill come not from Warren Road but from the Bridge Woods. When the swimming pool at Buckmore Park was being constructed, three Roman burials were found, lying in a row.[15] Earlier, in 1913, one had been discovered along Colepits Lane, a track which sloped down the steep bank (Colepits Bank) from the B2097 into the valley below.[23] It was probably the track along which the body of the unfortunate Emily Trigg was found. Much of it was destroyed when the M2 was constructed, but its eastern end still lies within Buckmore Park, passing adjacent the swimming pool. In 1913, it was being widened and the burial was found in its eastern bank. It consisted of a skeleton and two vases, one of which had been decorated with a yellow scroll. The skeleton was examined, and found to be that of an old man. The account does not indicate how far along the track the burial was found. If it was near the eastern end, it would seem to belong to the same group of burials as the other three.

We do not know why there were burials at this position. Was there a dwelling nearby? Miss Glover derives the name Buckmore from *bucca mere*, meaning a pool where buck drink.[24] The name is Anglo-Saxon, so it would seem that there were deer in Nashenden Valley when the

Jutes arrived. Fallow deer were brought to this country by the Romans, possibly so that they could create a park, or *saltus*, around each of their villas, as they did in their homeland.[25,26] The Medway valley was extensively settled, from Rochester to the enormous villa at Eccles and beyond. Did Nashenden Valley function as a deer park, or sort of country park-cum-game reserve? Were the burials those of resident game keepers? Or was the ridge, even in those days, forested and these were local woodsmen? We do not know, but in the absence of any explanation, I would like to think that these were local Blue Bell Hill residents who were eventually laid to rest at the head of the lovely valley which they must have known so well.

Flint arrow-heads from Mill Lane.
Courtesy of Mrs J Allonby.

Chapter Nine — References
Kits Coty
and other Antiquities

1)   Philp, B, **A Survey of the Medway Megaliths**. *Kent Archeological Review*, Vol 64, 1981.
2)   McCrerie, A, **Researches and Discoveries in Kent — Smythe's Megalith**. *Archeologia Cantania*, Vol LXX, 1956, p 251.
3)   Philp, B, *op cit* (See 1 above).
4)   Bibby, G **Testimony of the Spade**. Published 1957 by Collins.
5)   Drewett, P, Rudling, D, and Gardiner, M, **A Regional History of England. The South-East to AD 1000**. Published by Longman's Press.

6) Biggs, H, **The River Medway**. Published 1982, by Terence Dalton Ltd, Lavenham, Suffolk.

7) Jessup, F W, **Kent History Illustrated**, p 11. Published 1966 by KCC.

8) a) *Archeologia Cantania*, Vol XXI, 1895, p xlix.
    b) *Archeologia Cantania*, Vol XXV, 1902, p lx.
    c) Coles-Finch, W, **In Kentish Pilgrim Land**. Published 1925 by C W Daniel & Co.

9) Presnail, J, **Chatham**. Published 1952 by the Corporation of Chatham, p 16.

10) *Archeologia Cantania*, Vol CI, 1984, p 365.

11) Oral Information: Mrs J Allonby.

12) Rainbird Clarke, R, **Grime's Graves, Norfolk**. Published 1963 by HMSO.

13) Q/RDC/3 A-C Kent Archives Office. Burham Enclosure Award.

14) Cruse, R J, and Harrison, A C, **Excavations at Hill Road Wouldham**. *Archeologia Cantania*, Vol XCIX, 1983.

15) Records of the Lower Medway Archeological Research Group.

16) Charles, Thos, *Archeologia*, Vol 30, 1844, p 536.

17) Wright, Thos, *Archeological Journal*, 1844, pp 263–265.

18) *Victoria County History*, Vol iii, p 104.

19) Evans, A J, **On a late Celtic Urnfield at Aylesford**, *Archeologia* Vol 52, pp 315–388.

20) Kissick, E, **Roman Building on Blue Bell Hill**, *Kent Archeological Review*, No 102, 1990.

21) Charles, Thos, *Gentleman's Magazine*, 1842, p 532.

22) Witney, K P, **The Jutish Forest**, p 63. Published 1976 by University of London, Athlone Press.

23) *Archeologia Cantania*, Vol XXXI, 1915, p 281.

24) Glover, J, **Place-names of Kent**. Published 1976 by B T Batsford Ltd.

25) Stokoe, W J (compiled), **The Observer's Book of British Wild Animals**, p 162. Published by F Warne & Co.

26) White, J Talbot, **The Parklands of Kent**, pp 13–14. Published 1975 by A J Cassell Ltd, Sheerness.

Chapter Ten

Kits Coty Estate

We do not know what the area around Kits Coty looked like 4,000 years ago. It seems likely that the knoll on which the monument stands was cleared land, as excavating the ditch around it to obtain soil to construct the mound would have been severely hampered by the presence of trees. Miss Glover states that the name is derived from *ked coed*, meaning 'tomb in a wood', and hence is one of the few Kentish place-names based on the old Celtic language spoken by British tribes who preceded the Romans from about 600 BC. If her interpretation is correct, it suggests that the area became wooded, at least for part of the period. By Roman times, it may have been cleared again. On the western edge of Kits Coty field is a boundary ditch full of sarsen stones; FP 446 runs alongside it. Coles-Finch describes a well situated in or near this ditch: "On the west side of the field containing this old cromlech and in almost a direct line between it and Great Kewland ... is an elm tree and some stones of various sizes, beneath which is a well only some 2ft (0.6m) in diameter but tested to be 113ft (34.4m) deep." Coles-Finch thought this was a myth, until he was shown it by an old man who had known it since boyhood. It had "rough, large coping-stones".[2] The Romans are known to have dug deep wells to supply water for their sheep and cattle.[3] The area is not far from the enormous Roman villa at Eccles. There was another well at Great Culand itself, 180ft (54.8m) deep,[4] and yet a third was found in Salisbury Road when electricity cables were being laid in 1953.[5] The Romans may therefore have used the Downs as pasture.

The Romans were also given to terracing, and there are indications of this near Kits Coty.[3] *Kelly's Post Office Directory* of 1874[6] refers to "ancient military entrenchments" on the bank below the Maidstone–Chatham Road. Coles-Finch also describes terracing at this point and considers it to be old military works.[2] This seems unlikely. Entrenchments at this position, near the bottom of the Hill, would afford no protection from an enemy attacking from above. Further evidence of terracing is provided from old documents. A deed of exchange, dated 1744, refers to two parcels of land, one of three acres and one of 18 acres (7.3ha), known as The Cames, [7]and a title deed of 1832 refers to Gossey Cames and indicates that it was near or abutted Aylesford Common.[8] According to Richardson, *cam* meant an earth bank or a ridge on a hill.[8] In 1965, members of the Lower Medway Archeological Research Group surveyed the area and reported at least four terraces on the hill slope below the old A229.[10] The width of the terraces, which they did not consider to be natural, ranged from five to thirty yards (4.5m to 27.4m). A track ran along one of them. The Ordnance Survey Grid Reference which they gave, TQ 745616, locates them in the garden of White Lodge, where they can be seen by anyone walking along Kingswood Road, but they also extend south of Salisbury Road, one of them being crossed by the narrow path which originates at the junction of Russell Road with Queenswood Road, and runs upwards to the old A229 (the modern slip road). The Research Group considered that the terraces were associated with the Roman building on Warren Road. There are some steep alterations in ground level further west, towards Burham village. One of them, near the site of Great Culand, is crossed by FP 26. There is another nearer Burham village. Are these also the remains of Roman terracing?

From the Romans, if it was they who constructed the wells and terraces, we jump to the Middle Ages. Thorpe refers to a sword, and various weapons of undetermined age, being found in Kits Coty Field, and also to a spur, which had "a remarkably large rowel and the sprig on which it is fixed about half a foot [15cm] in length".[11] His father had been given a similar one many years before, from the same place. We can deduce that the spur dated from the 15th century. During this period, the armour worn by knights became very thick and heavy. Anyone who has seen Laurence Olivier's classic film of *Henry V*, may remember the scene before the battle of Agincourt (1415), in which the French knights are shown being hoisted on to their horses by cranes or derricks, rigged up for the purpose. Their armour was so thick and inflexible that they could hardly walk in it, let alone mount a horse. During the same period, horses' armour also increased in thickness, consequently the shank between the heel and the rowel of a knight's spur had to be lengthened if it was to reach through the horse's armour and prick its sides.[12] In passing, the war-horses of the 14th and 15th centuries had to carry such a large weight of armour, it is not surprising that they were antecedents of the shire horses that haul brewers' drays, such as can often be seen on holiday at Whitbread's Farm in East Peckham, than to breeds which today are used for riding.

By the 17th and 18th centuries, most land on the 'skirts' of the Downs was arable, as described by Thorpe in 1788.[11] Chalklin, writing of 17th century Kent, says that the enormous open fields were often divided into rectangular fields, called *shotts* or *shoots*. This was certainly true of land at the base of Blue Bell Hill. A description of Great Culand Farm in 1706 names three fields as Great Shott, Middle Shott and Upper Shott. Their areas ranged between 13 and 20 acres (5.2ha to 8ha).[13] Great and Middle Shotts were destined to be quarried away, when the second chalk pit was opened. The three were known collectively as Burham Shotts.[14,15] Confusingly, the field immediately north of Kits Coty Field was also known as Burham Shotts, even though it lay entirely within Aylesford parish. This field would eventually form the main part of Kits Coty Estate, bounded by Salisbury, Queenswood, Collingwood and Vincent Roads. By 1841, it was owned by Edward Prentis, of Tottington Farm, and occupied by Thomas Abbott, of Warren Farm (now Kits Coty Farm). Kits Coty Field itself is stated by Hasted to have been part of the demesne land of Tottington until the middle of the 18th century, when it was purchased by Mr Best, possibly after he purchased Great Culand.

By the end of the 19th century, Burham Shotts had been incorporated in Preston Hall Estates, as had Tottington. By 1906, Mr Brassey began to sell off Preston Hall Estates in preparation for moving from the district. He offered 'sitting tenants' the opportunity to buy their farms at concessionary prices. He had, however, other plans for Kits Coty. I am indebted to Mr White, of Little Kits Coty Farm, for much of the following information. The land was sold by auction. The advertising brochure reads:

SALE BY AUCTION IN A MARQUEE
ON KITS COTY ESTATE, MAIDSTONE, KENT.

This estate possesses beautiful views over the valley of the Medway, being no less than 500´ [152m] above sea level and has over three-quarters of a mile [1.2km] of frontage to the old Roman Road from Rochester to Chatham. 34 miles [54.7km] from London. Express trains to and from the city do the journey in 50 minutes and there are no less than 7 main line railway stations within easy reach of the estate. See particulars on other side.

SALE BY AUCTION IN A MARQUEE
ON THE ESTATE ON MONDAY MAY 18TH 1908.

Down train leaves Cannon Street, City,		11 am
Return ″ ″ Maidstone East		5.00 pm
		6.25 pm
		6.55 pm
		9.30 pm

Note:– All the plots, except where otherwise marked, are 20 ́ [6m] frontage and about 150 ́ [45.7m] deep; more than enough to build your own house and have a long garden in addition.

Building line:- 10 ́ [3m] back in respect of all plots except Shop Plots.

Remember we do not ask for all the money at once — only 2/- in the pound deposit then the balance in quarterly instalments. A very easy way of paying. Only 4 times each year. One plot costs you only 6d/week. You can, however, pay in full if you like and at once receive your free deeds.[16]

The plan which accompanied this brochure shows 884 building plots. Provision was made for shops in Salisbury Road and a hotel at the junction of Salisbury Road with Queenswood Road. On paper, the plan resembles nothing so much as a back-to-back tenement slum in a 19th century industrial town. Roads and plots covered not only the present Kits Coty Estate, but also a large area west of Kits Coty Farm. Fortunately for today's residents, Mr Joy, the tenant of Kits Coty Farm, purchased this western area, thus maintaining it as farmland, and a little later, in the 1920s, Mr White's parents gradually assembled sufficient of the main block of plots to constitute a viable farm. Known as Little Kits Coty Farm, it was primarily a dairy farm, supplying milk to the residents of the estate, and the surplus to Primrose and Len Dairies in Maidstone. During the 1939–1945 war, there was a national campaign to produce as much home-grown food as possible, thus releasing merchant shipping for other purposes. Allotment holders and gardeners were urged to 'Dig for Victory'. A prize was offered for the farm which achieved the greatest increase in its annual production; Mr White still proudly displays the award won by his parents on the 'Little' farm in 1941.

By 1932 there were about two dozen houses on the estate; some were substantial brick-built houses, while others were little more than weekend shacks, some surrounded by intensively cultivated gardens. Mrs Goodayle, who has known the estate since childhood, and has lived in Collingwood Road since her marriage in 1937, described life on the estate in the 1930s.[17] Land was cheap by modern standards; in 1934, her brother purchased two plots, each 40ft x 200ft (12.2m x 61m), for the princely sum of £25. Against this, tithe was still payable (1/– per year) even on housing plots. Newspapers were collected from the shop in Blue Bell Hill village. Groceries could be bought either from the Co-op at the corner of Robin Hood Lane, or from Mr White in Salisbury Road, who, as well as supplying milk as indicated above, sold groceries. He also sold paraffin. This was mainly used for lighting and heating by means of portable 'Valor' stoves. Most cooking was done on the kitchen range. Coal was not delivered to individual houses, as the unadopted roads were not suitable for heavy loads: it was dumped in Salisbury Road and householders had to wheel it from there in barrow-loads. Electricity would not reach the estate until 1953. There was a bus every ten minutes along the main road; return fares were 8d from Salisbury Road, or 6d from the Lower Bell. It was a thrifty age, so most people walked to the Lower Bell.

Rain water from the roof was collected in a square tank, placed at a suitable level to ensure gravity feed from tank to tap over the kitchen sink. Most of the houses were built in the 1930s, by which time early planning statutes were in force, consequently sewerage was mostly into cesspools. Before the 1939–1945 war, householders could apply for these to be emptied free of charge once a year. After the war, this was increased to once every six weeks; emptying additional to this was charged at 2/– per 100 gallons). The change resulted from the general improvement in living standards, one symptom of which was the installation of bathrooms, resulting in a much greater volume of waste water. Prior to 1939, few houses had bathrooms. The 'Saturday-night dip' took place in a metal bath, in front of the kitchen fire, the same water — topped up with 'hotters' from time to time — being used in succession by the whole family, usually in the order children, then Mum, then Dad. Refuse collection was non-existent. Newspapers were used to light the fire. Perishable rubbish, such as vegetable peelings, were either fed to the rabbits and chickens which many people kept, or composted and dug into the vegetable garden. Home-grown vegetables were an integral part of many household budgets. Tins and some bottles were buried. Plastic had not been invented, and jars were kept for home-made jams, chutneys, pickles and preserves, which were made by all self-respecting housewives. Fruit was usually plentiful: apples, pears, plums, currants, raspberries and gooseberries were grown in the gardens. Blackberries and damsons grew wild in the hedgerows. Wild strawberries were much more plentiful than they are now; children, with the time to look for them, and basing their search on knowledge of 'good' localities handed down from their older peers, could fill a pudding basin with them.

Before leaving Kits Coty Estate, let us look at the farm which also bears the name. It originated as part of Great Culand Farm, and hence was, and still is, in Burham parish. In 1706, Great Culand was sold by John Gunton and his sister Mary, to Thomas Hanch and his wife Elizabeth (*née* Thurston), who was a relative of Thomas Best, who financed the sale. The transaction was probably a marriage settlement on Elizabeth. The description of the farm includes "And also all that house or tenement called the Warren House and two pieces or parcels of land lying upon the Common called Burham Common conteyning [sic] by estimation two acres more or less with their appurtenances".[13] Seventy years later, Great Culand changed hands again, the Warren House now being described as " ... all that Toft or piece or parcel of land where-on there stood an old ruinous and decayed tenement called the Warren House with the parcel of land there-unto belonging called the Warren and two pieces of land there-unto adjacent and also one pasture close or field called the Common to the said premises belonging or apper-taining and therewith commonly demised, used and enjoyed situate, lying and being in the Parish of Burham".[18]

The term *toft* referred to a house or parcel of land on which a house has stood. Common rights could be associated with it, even though the house no longer existed. Both descriptions in the previous paragraph pre-date the enclosure of Burham Common, and indicate that piecemeal enclosure had been going on for a considerable time before the final enclosure of 1812–1815. In 1744, the house was occu-pied by one William Rayfield. By 1801, when Mudge drew his map, we find Warren House marked where Kits Coty Farm now stands, though whether it was still ruinous and decayed we cannot tell from the map. Certainly, by the time of the Tithe Map (1843), it seems to have taken on a new lease of life; the holding then consisted of a cottage, garden and yard, an arable field (Barn Field) of 48 acres (19.4ha), and two parcels, both marked 'Part of Common", one arable (four acres (1.6ha)) and one pasture (12 acres (4.8ha)). It was, by now, owned by Ed Prentis of Tottington, and occupied by Thos Abbott. Tottington was in Aylesford, but paid tithes to Burham. This was the result of the tithes having been granted to the monks of Rochester Priory by an earlier owner of Tottington in the 13th century.

The name, Warren House, gives a clue to the probable origin of the farm. Warrens in Kent were profitable. In some parts of the country, rabbits were killed as much for their fur as their meat, the black variety being particularly prized for the former. Wild black rabbits are rare nowadays, though they survive in a few places, such as Lundy Island in the Bristol Channel. Lambarde, in his *Perambulations*, commented that landowners in Kent did not bother to kill them for their skins since "Kent by the nearnesse to London hath so quick market of young rabbits that it killeth this game chiefly in summer".[19] There were strict laws against killing rabbits, or conies, to use the old name for the mature animals, and it seem likely that cottages were erected on the warrens for gamekeepers. These cottages were accompanied by small-holdings for the sustenance of their occupants. Mediaeval kings often granted 'Right of Free Warren' to their subjects for services rendered. Henry III, in 1238, granted right of free warren to Richard Grey and his heirs on their land at Aylesford. This may not have been such an honour as it seemed. The 'Beasts and Birds of the Warren' were the rabbit, hare, partridge and pheasant[20]. It is generally believed that rabbits were imported to England by the Normans, possibly from Spain. In Spain, semi-arid conditions restricted the growth of vegetation, and hence limited the size of rabbit populations. In England — rain-sodden, green England — there was no such restriction. Rabbits multiplied mightily. In 1310, the villagers of Ovingdean in Sussex, complained bitterly that conies from Ashdown Forest had 'annihilated' 100 acres of crops. Against this background, a grant of Free Warren, which permitted landowners to catch and kill rabbits, was as much a mediaeval pest-control measure as an honour. Successive kings made a virtue of necessity by conferring the right as though it were a special favour. Public relations is not a new art!

Chapter Ten — References
Kits Coty Estate

1) Glover, J, **Place-names of Kent**. Published 1982 by Meresborough Books, Rainham, Kent.
2) Coles-Finch, W, **In Kentish Pilgrim Land**, p 35. Published 1925 by C W Daniel Co, Graham House, Tudor Street, EC4.
3) Taylor, C, **Village and Farmstead**, p 84. Published 1983 by George Philip, 12–14 Long Acre, London.
4) Bergess, W and Sage, S, **Five Medway Villages**, p 17, Published 1983 by Meresborough Books, Rainham, Kent.
5) Oral information: Mr N White, Little Kits Coty Farm, Salisbury Road.
6) *Kelly's Post Office Directory*, 1874.
7) U480/T3 Kent Archives Office. Deed of Exchange. 29th January 1744.
8) U480/T17 Kent Archives Office. Indentures of Lease and Release. 11th June 1832.
9) Richardson, J, **The Local Historian's Encyclopaedia**, Entry A78. Published 1974 by Historical Publications Ltd, New Barnet.
10) O'Cock *et al*, *Archeologia Cantania*, Vol LXXX 1965, p 272, Lower Medway Archeological Research Group, Regional Survey Results for 1964-'65.
11) Thorpe, J, **Custumale Roffense**, pp 69-75. Published 1788.
12) Noel-Hume, I, **Archeology in Britain — Observing the Past**, p 97. Published 1953 by W & G Foyle, Ltd, London.
13) U234/T17 Kent Archives Office. Indenture of Sale, 21st February 1706.
14) U480/T3 Kent Archives Office. Deed of Exchange. 29th January 1744 (as 7 above).
15) P52/28/1 Deposition relating to Aylesford/Burham boundary.
16) Oral Information: Mr N White (as 5 above), who also kindly made available the original brochure of the auction.
17) Oral Information: Mrs Goodayle, Collingwood Road.
18) U234/T17 Kent Archives Office. Indenture of Lease and Release. 30th and 31st October 1778.
19) Lambarde, Wm, **A Perambulation of Kent**, Edition of 1826, p 5.
20) Garth Christian, **Ashdown Forest**, p 12. Published 1967 by the Society of Friends of Ashdown Forest.

Chapter Eleven
Soldiers on the Hill

For three-and-a-half centuries, Roman legions kept the peace in Britain, but at the end of the 4th century AD, they were recalled to defend their homeland, leaving the Romanised Britons to defend themselves against the incursions of Picts from Scotland, and Angles, Saxons and jutes from the continent. The well-known story of Hengist and Horsa dates from this period. Vortigern, or Wyrtgeorn, who was the leader of the Britons, sought the aid of mercenaries from the continent to repel the Picts. Hengist, and his brother Horsa, accepted the invitation, and dealt with the Picts very efficiently. Vortigern rewarded them with the gift of the Isle of Thanet. From there, they sent home to Jutland, in North Germany, for reinforcements. These having arrived, they emerged from Thanet, intent upon obtaining as much land as they could. This inevitably led to conflict with Vortigern. The battle took place in AD 455: the Jutes won, though Horsa was killed in the battle, as also was Catigern, the brother of Vortigern.

Modern historians question whether Hengist or Horsa were historical figures, or whether the names are mythical for unknown Jutish leaders. Whether this is so or not, it seems likely that a major battle took place, as both the *Ecclesiastical History*, compiled by the Venerable Bede in the 8th century, and the *Anglo-Saxon Chronicle*, dating from about the 13th century, specify a date and a place for it.[1,2] Antiquaries of the 17th and 18th centuries interpreted the location as Aylesford. Some of them were even more precise, saying that the battle was fought in the vicinity of Kits Coty.[3] This was based on a misunderstanding. They knew Kits Coty was old, but did not appreciate how old; they considered that the name derived from Catigern, and that the monument was his tomb. In fact, the Anglo-Saxon Chronicle did not refer to Aylesford, but to Aeglesthrep. It may, or may not, be significant that a survey of Boxley parish bounds in 1611 refers to an 'Aglesfield', on the boundary between Boxley and Bredhurst.[4] The Jutes had already sacked Canterbury, and were travelling westwards.

Whether they travelled along Watling Street, or whether they sailed round the coast, it is feasible that they moved inland through the great dry valleys that converge at Bredhurst, and there met Vortigern (See Map 6). Presnail inclines to the view that they reached Upchurch, and then deployed south through Meresborough: same idea, different valley[5]. The land south of Watling Street was settled in Roman times, and hence well supplied with roads. Whatever the truth of the matter, it seems possible that, on this occasion or another, via Bredhurst or some other route, Jutish warriors reached Blue Bell Hill. When Wright discovered the Roman building along Warren Road in 1844, he noted that the ruins were mixed with a few human bones and traces of burnt wood, and suggested that the building was "destroyed in the invasions of the barbarians which followed the retreat of the Romans".[6]

For 300 years after the Romans had gone, there was intermittent warfare, as Jutes, Angles and Saxons parcelled out the country between themselves. The Jutes retained Kent until AD 773, when Offa of Mercia defeated them at Otford, and chased them back to the Medway. Following this, the Kingdom of Kent merged with that of Wessex, though the Kentish people retained some of their peculiarly Jutish customs, including the custom of gavel-kind. This was a method of inheritance whereby a man's possessions were divided equally between all his children after his death, unlike the more widely practised primogeniture, by which the eldest son took everything. Even William the Conqueror did not eliminate gavel-kind, which persisted into the 20th century.

The next 250 years, between AD 780 and 1020, was the period of savage raiding by the Danes or Vikings. They first raided England in AD 787, and Kent in AD 832, announcing their arrival by arrival by ravaging the Isle of Sheppey. Their raids took place along the whole east and south coasts of England; they established themselves in Yorkshire, and gradually extended their sphere of influence down the east coast to Essex. Their raiding parties became larger. The first one, in AD 787, consisted of three ships. By the time of the battle of Fernham, referred to in Chapter Seven, they were no longer mere raiders, but an army on the move. They had 280 ships, each estimated to hold at least thirty men — a raiding force of 8,000. They were as much feared on the continent as they were in England. Although Haesten, following the battle of Fernham, failed to seize Kent, raids continued on the county for another 150 years. Whether their activities directly affected Blue Bell Hill, we do not know. They ravaged Rochester and west Kent in AD 999, Sandwich in AD 1009, Canterbury in 1011 and Sandwich again in 1013 and 1015. By this time, the Danes were led by Canute and the Saxons by Edmund Ironside. In AD 1016, they met at Otford. Edmund won the battle, and chased the Danes back to Sheppey, whether by boat or by the overland route which would have brought them up Blue Bell Hill we do not know. Edmund and Canute were so evenly matched that they agreed a truce, but a few months later Edmund died and Canute assumed the over-lordship of the whole country, Danes and Saxons. Following this, there was comparative peace for forty years.

In January 1066, Edward the Confessor died. Harold Godwinson was acclaimed king, though he was not of royal descent. There were other claimants to the throne, including Harold Hardrada, King of Norway, and William of Normandy — both Danes, as was Harold himself. In September, Hardrada landed in Yorkshire. Harold marched north to intercept him, and on September 25th defeated him at Stamford Bridge, eight miles from York, Hardrada being killed in the battle. Six days later, news reached Harold that William had landed at Pevensey, on the south coast between Eastbourne and Hastings. Harold and his men did a forced route march from York to London — approximately 200 miles in six days. He waited at London for four days, partly to rest and partly to give the *fyrd* — the local county militia — time to gather. On October 11th, he set out for Hastings, where William had set up camp.[7] His most likely route was via Watling Street to Rochester, then via the Roman Road — our road — to Hastings. He took two days on the journey, so may well have stayed overnight in this area, where he had good bases; Harold held the manor of Chatham, as well as the royal manor of Aylesford; his brother, Leofwin, held Burham, Nashenden and Leeds.[8] All of these are conveniently close to Penenden Heath, the traditional place of assembly in Kent. Some of the troops may have come down Blue Bell Hill on that fateful morning. We can imagine it, glowing in autumn glory, as they marched southwards, past where Maidstone now stands, over Linton Hill and on to their doom. They arrived at Senlac, where Battle now stands, in the evening of October 13th. Twenty-four hours later, Harold and his two brothers were dead, and William was conqueror of England.

There are no records of soldiers using the Hill for the next 600 years, at least not en masse, though no doubt plenty of individual knights, esquires and foot-soldiers passed along it. The next record which we have, however, was the biggest concourse of soldiers that Blue Bell Hill has ever seen. In 1648, England was at war with itself, immersed in that most desolating of all combats — a civil war. Cromwell and Parliamentarians fought King and Cavaliers. The people of Kent kept their

106

heads down and endeavoured to maintain business as usual. However, the established country gentlemen, the traditional administrators of the county, disliked the Committee which Parliament had set up to do this job. They drew up a petition and, in May 1648, set out for London to present it to Parliament, accompanied by a retinue of several thousand men. They were met at Blackheath by Fairfax, who prevented them from going any further. They returned to Rochester while Fairfax advanced to Meopham, where he left a small detachment to guard Watling Street while he took his main body of troops to East Malling. This was on May 31st.[7,9]

The Royalists spent the next day on Blue Bell Hill with their 10,000 troops. They were clearly visible to Fairfax. In a despatch after the battle, he stated that he "descried several thousand troops assembled on the bluff of the hill east of Kits Coty House".[9] This number must have spread over Burham and Wouldham Commons; they could not all have got on to the bluff. Their commander, George Goring, Earl of Norwich, despatched some 1,500 into Maidstone, these being apprentices, seamen and cavaliers with previous experience of fighting — his best troops. The rest remained on the Hill, strategically positioned to repel Fairfax whether he attempted to cross the river at Aylesford or at Maidstone. Fairfax did neither. Having camped at Malling for the night, on the morning of June 1st he marched his men smartly across Barming Heath, crossed the river at East Farleigh and advanced into Maidstone from the south, via Stone Street and Gabriel's Hill. His men were discovered by a reconnaissance party sent out by the Governor of Maidstone before they reached Stone Street, hence the townspeople were ready to defend themselves. Battle was joined at 7pm on the fine June evening; not until midnight did the townspeople surrender, in St Faith's churchyard. The battle for Maidstone was later described as "one of the most murderous conflicts of the war".[9]

The Earl of Norwich was old and, unlike Fairfax, had little experience of war. Refugees fleeing towards Blue Bell Hill brought him news of the battle, but he seems to have been slow to move. In fairness, getting 8,000 inexperienced men on the move could hardly have been accomplished in five minutes. By the time they were within two miles of Maidstone (about where the 'Running Horse' now stands) the refugees were reporting that the battle was over. The Earl retired discreetly to Rochester. Many years later, there was a curious little find, which leaves us wondering whether some of his troops also retired discreetly — possibly before the battle! Thorpe, writing in 1788, records that "Thomas Manley of Hall Place, Wouldham, dug a deep trench and raised a bank up the Common between Burham and Wouldham to confine the cattle to their respective commons. In digging the ditch the workmen found several war-like instruments of brass, some in the rude form of spear-heads, others like a cross with a peak at top and on one side, and on the other a hatchet after the manner of a pole battle-axe ..." These sound like the pole-axes of the 16th century, which were sometimes issued to hastily-mustered troops of the Civil War, in lieu of more up-to-date weapons. I have a mental picture of a group of men contriving to position themselves at the extreme western end of the main body of troops, quietly placing their weapons on the ground and then, one by one, melting into the landscape as the true countryman can do — especially if he is an experienced poacher! If I am wrong in my dating of the weapons, then there was at some time an unrecorded event on the Burham/Wouldham boundary which resulted in a number of weapons being left on the ground.

By 1652 England was at war with the Dutch. These wars included the famous episode of 1667, when the Dutch Admiral De Ruyter sailed his fleet up the Medway and attacked the ships anchored off Chatham Dockyard. Troops were stationed in Strood and Rochester to man the forts overlooking the River. Supporting horse troops were stationed in Maidstone. Locally, it was the period in which four soldiers "stealing conies in the Warren" shot the local farmer — an episode quoted by Vigar from the Aylesford Burial Register (1660).[10] The Warren was Cossington Warren, adjacent to Lower Warren Road. Later, following the accession of [Dutch] King William in 1689, England and the Netherlands became allies, and ganged up against their traditional enemy, France. The Dutch and English navies had complete control over the Channel, so there was little fear of invasion: most of the fighting was done on the continent. No doubt many soldiers passed up and down Blue Bell Hill; troop movements during the period of the French Wars may have contributed to pressure to turnpike the road at an early date. But now, mingled with the troops, were those pitiful relics of war — the wounded and destitute soldiers and sailors, for whom little or no provision was made. The Navy Board, in particular, was notorious for being in arrears with payments both to sailors and dockyard workers. It was during this period that the Accounts of the Overseers of the Poor of Aylesford Parish included such entries as:

1710 Gave to 11 seamen and 4 boys which came from France   3/6
1711 Gave to 8 seamen, all sick and lame   3/–
1711 Gave to 2 soldiers, one being blind   –/6d

108

In 1745, the attempt by Bonnie Prince Charlie to invade England from the north highlighted the need to modernise the militia. In times of special peril, when additional troops were required, it was still incumbent upon wealthy land-owners to provide and equip troops. However, the ordinary men, whom we would call conscripts, were not obliged to fight outside the limits of their own counties. This arrangement dated from Anglo-Saxon times. The problem which it posed for military commanders had surfaced during the Civil Wars, when the men of Kent firmly declined to cross the boundary into Surrey to fight for Cromwell, and, at about the same time, men from the West Country, who had come as far as Hampshire to support the King, announced that they were not going any further and made tracks for home.[7] Cromwell partly overcame it by setting up the first fully-professional, publicly-financed army that England had ever known, a move not too popular with some of his contemporaries. This, however, was only a nucleus. It still did not provide for an increase in militia in times of special threat. Consequently, in the middle of the 18th century, the Militia acts of 1757 and 1758 provided that the militia should be financed, clothed and equipped by central government, and should be subject to the same conditions of pay and service as the regular army. Its members would be liable to serve anywhere in England. The men of the militia were to be chosen by ballot, and were to serve three years, with regular attendance at training sessions. These Militia Acts were used during the War of American Independence, when it was feared that France, who supported the rebel colonies, might try to invade. They came into full force during the Napoleonic Wars of 1793–1815.

Although the names of those to serve were drawn by ballot, they were permitted to send substitutes — if they could find them! They also had to pay a fine directly to the army authorities, and a sum of money to the substitute, an arrangement which smacks strongly of legalised bribery. By 1793, the majority of substitutes were paupers from the workhouses. They, poor souls, had little choice in the matter. The Overseers of the Workhouse were expected to seek suitable work for the inmates and offer it to them; if an inmate refused the work he could be turned out of the workhouse. Obviously, the 'job' of substitute militia-man was considered suitable. We see the complete system at work in Aylesford in 1797, when the name of George Smith, Blacksmith, was drawn in the lottery. He paid twelve guineas to Colonel James, commander of the Western Kent Regiment of Militia, to find a substitute. He then swore on oath before a JP that he was "not possessed of an estate in lands, goods or money of the clear value of £500." The JP then authorised the Overseers of the Poor to pay him, George Smith, "half the current price paid for a volunteer in the County."[11b] Presumably this subsidy was based on the principle that the Overseers would no longer have to support the pauper in the workhouse. In 1797, the current price was £5; by 1803 it had increased to £15. Even paupers were in short supply as the number of Militia reached 11,000.

The fear of invasion reached its peak in 1803. In July, Mr Charlton was appointed Superintendent of Aylesford Parish, responsible for ensuring that instructions relating to defence and security were implemented — what we would now call Civil Defence. In October, he was instructed to erect a beacon on Blue Bell Hill, to be fired in time of need.[11b] This was the first record we have of a beacon on the Hill. The earlier system, set up to give warning of the Spanish Armada in 1588, did not involve Blue Bell Hill, all the beacons on this side of the river being on church towers (Burham, Wouldham, Aylesford, Boxley and Maidstone).[12] The beacon was about where the car park of the picnic area is now situated.[13] When the writer was a child, there was a small area at this location, as though someone had taken a gigantic spoon and scooped out a spoonful of the downs. This may have been the actual site of the beacon, giving it a flat base and some slight protection from the north-east wind. We used it for a highly dangerous game on bicycles, riding them down the vertical bank, bounding over the flat platform and finishing with a great sweep over the grass, going as near the edge of Culand Pit as we dared. The beacon remained in existence until at least 1812. According to Russell,[9] it was guarded by a detachment of six soldiers: a sergeant, a corporal and four privates. It is possible that advance preparations for the beacon led to the episode quoted by Goodsall, in which, some local woodsmen having caught a marten-cat, a hunt was arranged from the Upper Bell.[14] The marten was released, given 15 minutes to get away, and then tracked with beagles. It is unlikely that the woodsmen had beagles, but the soldiers may have suggested the idea to their officers.

Mr. Charlton also received instructions that "Aylesford is allotted to furnish 10 waggons with 2 men and 4 horses each which are to be numbered upon the front and marked BH. Upon the Beacons being fired these 10 waggons are to repair to the foot of Blue Bell Hill near the old Turnpike with 3 days provision for the men and their horses. Those teams who volunteer this service the Constable is not to impress for other service while they hold themselves in readiness for this occasion."[11b] The old Turnpike was Brick-on-Edge Cottage, at the junction of the Pilgrims' Way with the A229, established since 1739.[11c] What the men and their waggons were to do when they reached the foot of Blue Bell Hill we do not know. Napoleon never invaded so the arrangements were never put to the test.

In passing, we can note that, in happier times, another beacon was built at the same location. This was in 1935, as part of the Silver Jubilee celebrations of King George V, when a chain of beacons was set up over the whole country. The people on Burham Downs received their signal to light up when the beacon on Wrotham Hill was lit; Coxheath received their signal from Blue Bell Hill.

Since the Napoleonic Wars, the use of Blue Bell Hill by the army has been limited to training purposes. Twenty acres of Warren Farm were sold to the Board of Ordnance, probably about 1833.[11d] This may have been part of Frith Wood, where musket balls have been found, suggesting training exercises and manoeuvres.[15] In 1907, there were exercises stretching from Bredhurst, past Blue Bell Hill to Wouldham; these are fully described by Gulvin.[16] The main lesson emerging from the exercises was that the five forts intended to protect Chatham Dockyard from overland attack were unequal to the task, and were obsolete, even thought they had been completed only twenty-five years earlier. In the 1939–1945 war, rifle practice was carried out in Culand Pit. It was quite common, when going for a walk on the Downs, to find the red warning flag flying. A German 'plane crashed in Impton Wood, resulting in a small local resident, 11 years old, announcing to his mother, a little later in the day, that he was "the first publican on the scene". I have no wish to glorify war, that cruel destroyer of human lives and happiness, but *in memoriam* to all those, from Horsa, the son of Witta, the son of Wotan, to the young airmen of the 1940s who have died on or above the Hill, or have passed along the road on their way to death, I will end this chapter by quoting the poignant *Lament* of Wilfred Wilson Gibson:

"Lament"

We who are left, how shall we look again
Happily on the sun, or feel the rain,
Without remembering how they who went
Ungrudgingly and spent
Their lives for us loved too the sun and rain.

A bird among the rain-wet lilac sings —
But we, how shall we turn to little things
And listen to the birds and winds and streams
Made holy by their dreams,
Nor feel the heart-break in the heart of things.

Chapter Eleven — References
Soldiers on the Hill

1) Bede, **Ecclesiastical History**. Edited by J A Giles. Published 1907 by George Ball & Sons.
2) Compilers, **Anglo-Saxon Chronicle**. Edited by J A Giles. Published 1907 by George Ball & Sons.
3) Thorpe, J, **Custumale Roffense**. Published 1788.
4) Cave-Brown, Arthur, **Notes about Boxley**. Published 1870 by Wickham, Week Street.
5) Presnail, James, **Chatham. The Story of a Dockyard Town**. Published 1952 by Corporation of Chatham.
6) Wright, *Archeological Journal*, 1844. Pp 263–264.
7) Blaxland, Gregory, **South-east Britain — Eternal Battleground**. Published 1981 by Meresborough Books, Rainham, Kent.
8) Compiled, **Domesday Book**. Published 1983 by Phillimore & Co, Ltd.
9) Russell, J M, **The History of Maidstone**. Published 1881. Reprinted 1978 by John Hallewell, Rochester.
10) Vigar, J E, **History of Aylesford Parish Church**. Published 1982, Kent Archives Collection.
11) Kent Archives Office, Sundry Documents:
    a) P/12/12/2 Aylesford Parish. Accounts of Overseers, 1705-1712
    b) P12/17/1-5 Aylesford Parish. Instructions to Superintendent, Napoleonic Wars.
    c) U/1087/01 Estate Papers of the Fowle family.
    d) U/886/T1 Estate Papers of Preston Hall.
12) Lambarde, William, **Perambulation of Kent**. 2nd Edition.
13) *Maidstone Journal and Kentish Advertiser*, 5th May 1812. Public notice re proposed Enclosure Award Roads on Burham common, making reference, inter alia, to the position of the beacon.
14) Goodsall, Robert, **A Fourth Kentish Patchwork**. Published 1974 by Stedehill Publications, Harrietsham, Kent.
15) Oral information: Mrs J Brennan.
16) Gulvin, K R, **Chatham's Concrete Ring**. Published 1979 by Medway Military Research Group.

Chapter Twelve
Ponds, Paths and Place-names

Ponds

It is not generally realised how many ponds there are, or were, on the Hill. Some are still in existence. Some have been filled deliberately so that little or no trace remains of them. Some have silted up, but are still recognisable as depressions in the ground. What do we know of the construction, uses and ages of these ponds? The best known ones are those associated with the older buildings, such as Cossington Fields Farm, the Robin Hood Pub and Robin Hood House. The latter, on the Tithe Map, had two ponds, one each side of the road. The one adjacent to the house still exists as an ornamental pond.

Dew ponds are traditionally said to be lined with clay and straw

113

Plate 21   *Cynthia standing by the pond at the top of Warren Road. Note the marker oak in the background.*

or brushwood, weighted down with stones[1]. One, at least, had this construction. This was the one which now lies along Impton Lane, opposite the junction with Galena Close. During the 1930s, the resident who built the house called 'Outlands' dug out the pond to obtain the accumulated leaf mould for his garden. In later years, he would describe how he found a layer of stones and brushwood below the leaf mould.[2] The pond in Impton (see Chapter Six) probably had the same construction; it certainly had a layer of stones at its base. A stick, driven down 12 to 15 inches (30 to 38cm) through the accumulated debris would hit stones, no matter whereabouts in the pond it was inserted. I have no information on any of the others, but there is no reason to think that they have, or had, any different construction.

What of their ages? It has been said that most dew ponds date from the 18th century, though it is acknowledged that some are older and may be prehistoric.[1] One of ours, at least, was older than 18th century. This was the one which lay immediately north and west of the wireless mast compound at Cossington Fields. A survey of Boxley Parish Bounds, taken in 1611, shows that it was a boundary mark between Boxley and Aylesford Parishes.[3] If it was serving as a boundary mark in 1611, it had probably served the same purpose since the boundaries were defined, which leads us to the conclusion that it was an ancient pond. Regrettably, it was filled in during the 1960s, though its 'marker tree' still persists (see below). Examination of *Map 5* will show three ponds in a row on the boundary between Aylesford and Burham parishes. One lay at the south-western corner of Podkin Meadow; it is now visible only as a shallow depression covered in scrub. One further north, on the western edge of Podkin Wood, has now been incorporated into a small amenity area to serve the development along Laurie Gray Avenue. The third, at the back of St Alban's Church, was a larger shallower depression in the ground but was destroyed by the M2 widening scheme.

Some of the ponds were carefully shaped, the bank on one side being almost vertical, while that on the other side sloped, thus permitting animals to obtain access to the water. Impton and Cossington Fields ponds both showed this feature. In one of two ponds in the woods bordering the southern edge of Jack Barling's Meadows, which were obliterated by major tree-felling in 1986–87, the sloping side was replaced by a clearly defined, slightly curving path. I do not know its age, though it is shown on the Tithe Map of 1843. Some of the ponds have a large tree beside them, usually an oak. The best example of this is the pond at the junction of Mill Lane with Warren Road, where a truly venerable oak stands beside the pond (see *Plate 21*). Cossington Fields Pond was marked by an equally ancient tree, Impton by a less ancient one. I have noticed the same thing in other parts of the country, for example in north Gloucestershire, which leads me to wonder why ponds had 'marker' trees. Is it, perhaps, the last trace of some religious belief, which required the god or goddess of the pond to be provided with a tree for a dwelling?

Paths

Local walkers will know that some of our paths are deeply sunken, especially those on the steepest part of the downs (see *Plate 22*). The obvious explanation is that centuries of use have worn them away, but I find this explanation unsatisfactory, for two reasons:
1. It implies that they originated as paths. Now, our ancestors were not stupid. They must have known, as we do, that a path which runs straight up a hill has the steepest possible gradient. If the sunken paths originated as paths we would expect them to slant. A few do, such as BW22, known to be an ancient drove road, and later confirmed as an enclosure award road, but most plunge down the hillside at right angles to the contours. Others lie on the sides of spurs of the downs, where walking would have been difficult, as one foot would have been constantly at a higher level than the other.

Plate 22   Sunken path on Burham Downs (FP 24).

2. A few of the sunken paths are not on the scarp slope, but below it, on a much more gentle gradient where we would not expect erosion to be very marked. Indeed, there is one at Eccles, south-east of Rose Cottage, which lies almost parallel to the contours.

So what other explanation of their origin might there be? Ditches or dykes were commonly used as boundaries, in Kent as in the rest of southern England.[4] They are found in old deer parks, such as Lulling-stone.[5] There is a well-known one at Chislehurst, separating Petts Wood from adjacent common land. Reference was made in Chapter Eleven to Mr Manley's attempt to dig a ditch and raise a bank between Wouldham and Burham Commons. His fellow commoners seem to have mistrusted his motives as they took him to the next Court-leet (manorial court), where he was fined £5 and ordered to fill the trench. Whether he actually did so is open to question, as in 1862, when Wouldham Common was enclosed, the Commissioners of Enclosure had first to define the boundaries of the common, and they found that it was in part defined by a deep ditch.[6,7] So, might some of our sunken paths have originated as boundary ditches? Certainly some of them functioned as boundaries. The sunken part of FP24, from Common Road to Great Culand, lay at the eastern edge of Burham Common. FP442, from Warren Road to the footbridge on Blue Bell Hill, marked the edge of Common Waste Hill. The lower part of this path was destroyed when the new A229 was

116

constructed, but the upper part still exists. On the downs between the A229 and modern Boxley Hill are three deep dykes, parallel to each other and evenly spaced about 300 yards apart. They marked the edges of Boarley and Tyland Warrens.[8] The most easterly of the three is occupied by footpath KH29. The other two are not rights of way: I know of them because as children we roamed freely through these woods. Mr Merrett, whose family lived at Cossington Fields Farm for many years, stated that they were used by farm occupants.[9]

Dykes not lying on the escarpment include the one at the western edge of Kits Coty Field; that lying immediately east of Impton Pond, and approximating to the boundary between the land holdings of Mr Best and Mr Corrall, and one now occupied by the steps from Marlow Copse to Sherwood Avenue. Prior to the developments of the 1970s, this was about 4ft (1.2m) deep and 5ft (1.5m) wide, and marked the boundary between Boxley and Chatham parishes. There are traces of one in Tunbury Bottom, where it would have formed the boundary between Impton and Boxley parish. So, there is evidence that sunken paths and boundaries coincided. Which came first, we cannot tell. Existing paths may have been used as boundaries, and either became eroded or were dug out to become dykes. Alternatively, ancient boundary ditches may have been used as paths. If they were deliberately dug, soil thrown out would originally have formed banking or mounding adjacent to them, and there are traces of this at some points, but it would require a properly conducted 'dig' to determine the matter beyond doubt. Unless and until we can persuade a tame archaeologist to investigate our sunken paths, we can only speculate on their origins and ages. They may not all be the same age or have the same origins. But when next you toil up the deep, steep path, out of the wind and away from the noise of modern traffic, spare a thought for those who, unknown years ago, may have dug out the great V-shaped trench with primitive picks and shovels. And, if you see their ghosts sitting quietly eating their lunch, don't disturb them. They earned their rest.

Roads

In early days, when all travel and transport was by foot or pack-horse, there was little if any difference between paths and roads, with the exception of the great military roads built by the Romans and the minor roads which branched from them. Some of these survived and some did not. At the bottom of Blue Bell Hill, a minor road led towards Boxley; the western end of it is no longer a right of way, and is now marked only by a line of trees. The eastern end of it persists as a footpath, emerging in Boxley at the significantly-named Street Farm, and continuing in a straight line past Boxley Church to Detling.[10] Lower Warren Road, which Coles-Finch considers was a pack-way[11] became upgraded to the status of King's Highway. The 1611 survey of Boxley parish bounds refers to it as such, and names it as Flinty-wall Way.[12] It was at that time the main road between Aylesford and Lidsing. The accounts of the Aylesford Parish Surveyors list expenditure on it, indicating that it was recognised as a public highway.[13] The chalk bank overlooking it was Cossington Warren, hence the name of the road and of the farm, situated part way along it, and of which a shed and a mounting-block survive. The latter has been removed, but possibly survives awaiting re-instatement. In 1710, the Overseers of the Poor of Aylesford Parish:

> *Gave to a woman and three children sick with smallpox in Fowls*
> *barn 4 days to get her gone ... 2/6 (£3)*

This barn was probably part of Warren Farm, which was occupied by the Fowle family during the 18th century.[14]

Finally, the Pilgrims' Way. This forms the southern boundary of our study area. The name is modern, dating from the 19th century. Belloc, in 1904, postulated a prehistoric route connecting the Kent coast with Salisbury Plain and Stonehenge, which later served as a pilgrim route between Winchester and Canterbury.[15] This caught the public imagination, but already by 1925 it was being questioned. Recently, Turner has reviewed the evidence, and concludes that there is little evidence of a through route in prehistoric, Roman or mediaeval times.[16] He acknowledges that lengths of road may have existed along the foot of the downs, but considers that these were of varying dates and origins, and did not constitute a continuous long-distance route. Of the possible origins which he and others have suggested, two would seem applicable to our section of it:

1. Turner observes (p2) that in many places the Pilgrims' Way follows the cultivation line. This is true between Blue Bell Hill and Detling. Where cultivation extends north of the track, this is a recent development (mostly post-1939).

2. Elliston Erwood suggested that sections of it may have originated as roads along which chalk was transported from the pits, and refers to the 'building boom' of the Middle Ages.[17] With an alteration in date of 1,000 years, we can possibly apply the idea to our stretch of it. The Medway Gap was heavily settled in Roman times; they would have needed chalk or lime for their famous mortar. Perched above Wouldham is Scarborough Farm. Miss Glover interprets the name as 'stronghold by a cleft or gap', and refers to the existence of the chalk pits.[18] The name, however, is Jutish, so if the 'scar' does refer to the chalk pit then it must have already existed when the Jutes arrived, and must have been conspicuous enough to give a name to the area. Did the Romans quarry chalk there? Did they construct a road to haul the chalk towards the river, either to a wharf or to a road following the line of the river towards Rochester? Did they also extend the road eastwards towards the enormous Roman villa at Eccles? It would explain the names Burham Street and Street Farm.

There is an obvious gap in the continuity of the Pilgrims' Way at Culand. I do not propose to hypothesise about it, as it seems more relevant to a history of Eccles or Burham than of Blue Bell Hill. If anyone wishes to explain why the modern road does such an appallingly dangerous wiggle immediately west of Bull Lane, the explanation will have to take account of:

a) The effects of quarrying;
b) "All the Forestalls lying nere and belonging to" Great Culand;[19]
c) Why the parish boundary no longer crosses the road as it did prior to 1773;[20]
d) Why the parish boundary follows the road for a short distance between Culand and Hale Farm, this being the only place where the boundary coincides with a road.

Place-names

I have given the origin of some place-names and field-names in the text, but not all. Place-names can change out of all recognition over the centuries, so that we can not be certain of their origins unless early records are available. On the other hand, I see no harm in speculating, provided we make it clear that we are only speculating. With this proviso, let us look at some of the field-names on Blue Bell Hill.

Up Court and Court Hall

Up Court was the field bounded by Lower Warren Road, the Roman Road and the slip road below the Lower Bell. Court Hall was opposite the Lower Bell, and sloped down to the Pilgrims' Way.[21] The similarity of name suggests that, before the Turnpike Trustees diverted the main road, these two were one field. The name court commonly has one of two meanings. It may stem from *curt*, meaning short (we still talk of a curt answer, or of curtailing discussion), or it may, literally, mean court. It seems unlikely that a field stretching from the Roman Road to the Pilgrims' Way would qualify to be called a short field. We can, therefore, speculate whether this was, in times long past, the place at which the Hundred Courts were held in the Lathe of Aylesford. It is strategically positioned on the Roman Road, with branch roads leading towards Boxley, Burham, Eccles and the river crossing at Aylesford. If we are correct in thinking that the shoulder of the hill above the Lower Bell was part of Aylesford Common (see *Maps 1* and *3*), then the field was adjacent to the common and may, indeed, have formed part of it. Since the Hundred Courts were held every month, the land on which they were held was unlikely to have been available for cultivation. Richardson states that Hundred Courts usually began in the open air, at a place distinguished by a landmark, such as a cross-roads or barrow[22]. Court Field lies in the middle of the group of barrows at the foot of the hill, and, indeed, the original White Horse Stone lay at its southern corner.

The term hall applied to the lower portion of the field may have derived from hale, meaning a corner (see Chapter Three). The corner, in this case, had been physically cut off by the new Turnpike Road.

Kits Coty

This is the oldest name on the hill. According to Miss Glover, it stems from *ked coed*, meaning tomb wood.[23] If this is correct, then the name is Celtic in origin, in other words it is derived from the language spoken by the Britons before the Romans arrived. Celtic survived in the west country, where it gave rise to Welsh and the old Cornish languages. Holiday-makers in Wales may have visited Bettws-y-Coed — 'the Fall in the Wood'. It is one of only a handful of names in Kent which are Celtic in origin, others being some of the river names (e.g. Darenth, Cray, Lympne, possibly Medway in part), and the name of Kent itself. If Miss Glover's derivation is correct, it suggests that at sometime during the five or six centuries before the Romans arrived, the spur on which Kits Coty stands became wooded.

Kit Hill

Strangers to the area often confuse this with Kits Coty, expecting to find it near the foot of the downs. In fact, there is no connection between them. The present Kit Hill Avenue was a Brake Estate road (see Chapter Three), originally called Alexandra Road, at the northern extremity of Aylesford parish. Most of the road is over the boundary in Chatham. The present name is derived from Kite Hill, which is included in accounts for tree-felling between 1709 and 1713,[24] and, according to the Aylesford Tithe Map, included the area now occupied by Montfort Road.

The kite is one of our biggest birds of prey, with a wing span of five feet. Although now confined to a small area in Wales, in past centuries it was widely distributed. Like most of the hawks, it spends long periods soaring in circles, using up-currents of air to keep itself aloft without expending much energy in wing movements. Kite Hill, perched on the ridge separating Taddington Valley from Walderslade Bottom, must have been ideal for this; from almost any direction, the wind would hit the sides of a valley and be converted into an up-draught.[25]

Kites nest in trees; being so large, they require large trees, preferably oaks, and build their nests very near the trunk. Their food includes moles, rats, mice, voles, snakes and birds such as partridges, all of which are characteristic of fairly open ground, including corn-fields. We can, therefore, deduce that when Kite Hill acquired its name — we do not know when this was — there were both large trees and cultivated land in the vicinity.

Impton

The possible derivation of this name has already been considered. We can, however, briefly consider the spelling Impeton, as given in the list of charters quoted by Richardson (Chapter Six, Reference 4). According to Cameron, in the early Anglo-Saxon period many names were preceded by *aet* (modern *at*), which took the dative case.[26] The Anglo-Saxon dative singular ending most frequently found in place-names was *–e*. With time, the prefix *aet* was dropped, but the dative form survived in the place-name. This could explain the *e* in Impeton: it was originally *aet Impe* (at the plantation). If this is the correct explanation, then the name originated fairly early in the Anglo-Saxon period.

Podkin Meadow

This is one of the few parcels of land on the hill whose name has remained in everyday use. The earliest reference to the name which I have found is dated 1744, though it related to the wood and not the meadow, and was spelled Potkin.[27] In the Tithe Assessments 100 years later, the wood is still Potkin, the meadow is named as Poakin.

In 1773, it is noted in the Accounts of the Overseers of the Poor of Aylesford Parish that land held by Ed Fowle was previously held by Wm Bodkin.[28] The Accounts give the names of the landholders who were responsible for paying the rates, but only rarely do they name the land itself. Consequently, we cannot be certain which land Bodkin occupied, but we can tell from the general context, that is was somewhere on Blue Bell Hill. The ending *–kin* is unusual in place-names. It is possible — we cannot put it more strongly than that — that Podkin is a corruption of the personal name Bodkin. If this is not the origin of the name, then we need to consider whether the prefix *pot–* indicated that ancient pottery or potsherds had been found in the ground, though remembering that the name originally applied to the wood, not the meadow, and most of the wood is now built on by the Crematorium.

Failing either of these derivations, then it is probably one of the names which has changed unrecognisably over the centuries. It seems rather prone to change, as evidenced by the variants Potkin, Podkin and Poakin, while a friend who lived in the area in the 1930s knew it as Tonkins!

Telegraph Field

I was puzzled to find this name on the Burham Tithe Map and Assessment. It was a two-acre field fronting onto Common Road, where the water tank now stands, and the slip road emerges. Tucked into the corner of it, opposite where the beacon stood (see Chapter Eleven), was a cottage and garden, named simply 'Telegraph etc.' I knew of no telegraph systems, other than the naval ones along the Thames Estuary and the North Kent Coast, but eventually succeeded in tracking down the story of Blue Bell Hill's Telegraph. I shall now use this little snippet of history to bring my history of Blue Bell Hill to a close.

Since at least mediaeval times, beacons had been used to spread warning of danger. As generalised red alerts, they were adequate, but as a means of conveying specific information, they left much to be desired. Between 1790 and 1815, both the French and the English experimented with methods of sending messages. Early telegraph systems used shutters bearing letters by which messages could be literally, if laboriously, spelled out. This was superseded by the semaphore, which was rather like a railway signal with two or three arms; different positions of the arms coded for different letters of the alphabet. (Guides and Scouts used to learn this system, using their own arms instead of mechanical ones.) Parallel with this was the development of codes of two or three letters to indicate standard messages, such as "Ship in Distress". The universal 'SOS' signal remains to this day.

By 1795, the Admiralty had established a line of telegraph stations between London and Deal, with a branch line to Sheerness Dockyard. It is said that, at its peak, a message could be transmitted from London to Deal in seven minutes.[29] These stations employed the shutter system. They were decommissioned in 1814, following the defeat of Napoleon, only to be hastily recommissioned six months later when he escaped from Elba. After his final defeat at Waterloo, the Admiralty modernised their lines of communication to the coast, and added additional ones to the Dockyards at Portsmouth and Devonport. They used semaphores instead of shutters, and altered the positions of some of the stations near London. In Kent, their new line converged with the older one at Gad's Hill, hence the name Telegraph Hill at Higham.

The commercial world now became interested in semaphores. In 1825, Liverpool Dock Trustees were authorised by Act of Parliament to set up telegraph stations between Liverpool and its nearby ports as part of their improvement plan for the docks. The design of this telegraph system was entrusted to one B L Watson, a colourful figure who signed himself 'Lieut. RN'. About 1840, he departed from Liverpool, pursued by accusations that his name was not on the official Admiralty Lists, and that he had 'pinched' his ideas on telegraphs from someone else. He took up residence in London, and set up "Watson's General Telegraph Association". This company advertised its services in shipping publications, stating that any vessel registered on the company's telegraph list would be reported as it passed each station, so that owners were kept informed of its progress. The registration fee was £1 per annum.

To avoid the fog of the Thames Estuary, Watson established his line of stations further south than the Admiralty's line. Starting from the company's office at Topping Wharf, Southwark, the line went to Sydenham Hill (where the Crystal Palace would later be built), then to Knockholt Beeches, Wrotham Hill, Blue Bell Hill, Chatham, Barrow Hill, Whitstable, etc. The Admiralty used his services, paying him 10 shillings a message, but the enterprise was short-lived. A fire at Toppings Wharf destroyed the company's office and central telegraph in 1843. It was never re-established. Increasing smog in London and the Thames Estuary was rendering visual communication systems difficult, and the invention of the electric telegraph was about to render them obsolete. By 1849, the Admiralty was in electric communication with the Admiralty Office at Portsmouth.

Ponds, Paths and Place-names

1)   Richardson, J, **Local Historian's Encyclopaedia**. Entry E32. Published 1974, Historical Publications Limited, New Barnet.
2)   Oral information: Mr A Olley, Tunbury Avenue.
3.   Cave-Brown, J, **Notes About Boxley**. Published 1870, Wickham, Week Street, Maidstone.
4)   Hoskins, W G, **The Making of the English Landscape**, p 27. Published 1955 by Hodder & Stoughton.
5)   Pittmen, S, **Lullingstone Park**. Published 1983, Meresborough Books, Rainham.
6)   Thorpe, J, **Custumale Roffense**, p 73 onwards.
7)   Q/RDC/25 Kent Archives Office. Wouldham Enclosure Award.
8)   U234/E21 Kent Archives Office. Aylesford Estate Papers.
9)   Oral information: Mr R Merrett, Cossington Fields Farm.
10)   Margary, I D, **Roman Roads in the Weald**. Published 1949 by Phoenix House.
11)   Coles-Finch, W, **In Kentish Pilgrim Land**, p 167. Published 1925.
12)   Cave-Brown, J, **Notes About Boxley**. Published 1870, Wickham, Week Street, Maidstone.
13)   P/12/12/2 Kent Archives Office. Accounts of the Overseers of the Poor of Aylesford Parish.
14)   U886/T1 Kent Archives Office. (Bundle 14) Preston Hall Papers.
15)   Belloc, H, **The Old Road**. Published 1904.
16)   Turner, D J, **The North Downs Trackway**. *Surrey Archeological Collections*, Vol LXXII, 1980.
17)   Elliston-Erwood, F C, **The Pilgrim's Way, its antiquity and its alleged mediaeval use**. *Archeologia Cantania*, Vol XXXVII.
18)   Glover, J, **Place-names of Kent**. Published 1982, Meresborough Books, Rainham, Kent.
19)   U234/T17 Kent Archives Office. Indenture of Sale, 21st February 1706.
20)   P52/28/1 Kent Archives Office. Deposition by Abraham Overy re. boundary between Aylesford and Burham parishes. 13th December 1773.

21) CTR/12/A and CTR/12/B Kent Archives Office. Aylesford Tithe Map and Assessment.
22) Richardson, J, **Local Historian's Encyclopaedia**. Entry B39. Published 1974, Historical Publications Limited, New Barnet.
23) Glover, J, **Place-names of Kent**. Published 1982, Meresborough Books, Rainham, Kent.
24) U480/E49Kent Archives Office. Estate Papers of the Best Family.
25) Rev. Johns, C A, Edited W Alexander, **British Birds in their Haunts**. Published 1961, revised edition, 1948 Routledge & Kegan Paul.
26) Cameron, K, **English Place-names**, pp 30-31. Published 1961, B T Batsford Ltd.
27) U480/T3 Kent Archives Office. Deed of Exchange, 29th January 1744.
28) P12/12/2 Kent Archives Office. Accounts of the Overseers of the Poor, Aylesford Parish, 1773.
29) Hardy, Miss A G, **The Old Telegraph from London to the Coast of Kent**. *Archeologia Cantania*, Vol XLIV, 1932, p 211.
30) Wilson, G, **The Old Telegraphs**, Chapter 6. Published 1976, Phillimore & Co Ltd.